FOLLOWING CHRIST

FOLLOWING CHRIST

Faith and Life Series

Third Edition

BOOK SIX

Ignatius Press, San Francisco

Catholics United for the Faith, Steubenville, Ohio

Nihil Obstat:	Reverend James M. Dunfee
	Censor Librorum
Imprimatur:	+ Most Reverend Bishop R. Daniel Conlon
	Bishop of Steubenville

Director of First Edition: The late Rev. Msgr. Eugene Kevane, Ph.D.
Assistant Director and General Editor of First Edition: Patricia Puccetti Donahoe, M.A.
First Edition Writer: Joseph C. DiCarlo, Jr., M.A.
Director and General Editor of Revision: Caroline Avakoff, M.A.
Revision Writer: Colette Ellis, M.A.
Revision Artist: Christopher J. Pelicano

Catholics United for the Faith, Inc. and Ignatius Press gratefully acknowledge the guidance and assistance of the late Reverend Monsignor Eugene Kevane, Director of the Pontifical Catechetical Institute, Diocese of Arlington, Virginia, in the production of the First Edition of this series. The First Edition intended to implement the authentic approach in Catholic catechesis given to the Church through documents of the Holy See and in particular the Conference of Joseph Cardinal Ratzinger on "Sources and Transmission of Faith." The Revised Edition and Third Edition continue this commitment by drawing upon the *Catechism of the Catholic Church* (Libreria Editrice Vaticana, © 1994, 1997).

The Subcommittee on the Catechism, United States Conference of Catholic Bishops, has found this catechetical text to be in conformity with the *Catechism of the Catholic Church*.

2015 reprint
See www.faithandlifeseries.com for a list of minor textual changes
as well as additional tools and resources
© 1987, 2004, 2011 Catholics United for the Faith, Inc.
All rights reserved
ISBN 978-1-58617-568-9
Manufactured by Friesens Corporation
Manufactured in Altona, MB, Canada in March 2015
Job # 210776
in compliance with the
Consumer Protection Safety Act

Contents

THE LAST THINGS

CHRISTMAS SEASON SUPPLEMENT

A Note to Parents

Dear Parents,

The *Faith and Life* series was originally published in 1984. The book you hold in your hands is one of over 4.6 million books sold since then. From the beginning, the series was intended to provide schools, parishes, and families with the catechetical tools and essential elements of Catholic doctrine pivotal in the formation of young Catholics.

While the doctrine and Tradition of the Church remain essentially unchanged, as time has passed the editors have provided additional teaching tools that enrich the series and make it even more accessible to all types of students. Since its introduction, the series has seen the addition of activity books, teacher's manuals, numerous online resources, scriptural quotations, and correlations with the *Catechism of the Catholic Church*. Additionally, this edition has been updated to incorporate the new translations of the Roman Missal introduced into the Mass during Advent 2011. These additions were all undertaken with an eye toward the *General Directory for Catechesis'* statement: "It is necessary that religious instruction in schools appear as a scholastic discipline with the same systematic demands and the same rigor as other disciplines. It must present the Christian message and the Christian event with the same seriousness and the same depth with which other disciplines present their knowledge" (GDC, 73; Congregation for the Clergy, 1998).

In this sixth grade student text, *Following Christ*, you will find that emphasis has been given to the scriptural basis of our Faith in accord with Sacred Tradition. Every chapter opens with a Scripture passage, and important verses supplement the text where relevant. Each chapter closes with questions and answers based on Church teaching as found in the *Catechism of the Catholic Church*. Vocabulary words are indicated in bold type and in the Words to Know sections. Their definitions are found in the glossary. Common Catholic prayers are also taught in the lessons, and presented at the end of the book.

It is important to realize that, as parents, you are the primary educators of your child. Your active participation in your child's religious education is highly encouraged by the Church. As a family, you are the first witnesses of God's love to your child. If you provide a model of Catholic living at home, if as a family you participate in the sacramental life of the Church, and if you pray and attend Mass together, your child is more likely to take to heart the lessons he will learn in religion class. Family discussions of current events with a healthy religious perspective will allow your child to grow up with a better understanding of the world around him, and more importantly, help him to be a true Catholic and follower of Christ in the midst of it. As stated in the *General Directory for Catechesis*, "family catechesis precedes . . . accompanies and enriches all forms of catechesis" (GDC, 226). Providing your child with a strong Catholic identity at an early age, while not ensuring a lifetime of devotion, will certainly prepare him for the challenge of becoming a faithful Catholic adult.

We encourage you to use the *Following Christ* student text, along with its resources, to assist you in the task of sharing the Good News with which you have been entrusted. More information and resources can be found at www.faithandlifeseries.com.

We sincerely hope that this series will provide parents, catechists, and teachers with the assistance they need in the task of evangelizing young people and of putting them in "communion and intimacy with Jesus Christ" (GDC, 80).

INTRODUCTION

Jesus has promised that he will be with us to the end of the world. He is with each of us, personally, in every step of our life. What is the special ingredient that Jesus adds to life that changes it from a dull chore to a rich adventure? The special ingredient is love. Jesus tells us that he came so that we "may have life, and have it abundantly" (Jn 10:10).

How do we receive this abundant life that Jesus wants to give us? We receive it by following the plan that God has for us. Before you build a house you need a blueprint. Even God, before he made the first man, had a plan for his body and soul—he planned every bone and every muscle, every nerve, every organ, every blood cell. We have a plan to lay the foundation of our lives: God's law.

Law is necessary if we are to have order in life, and without order there can be no happiness. All life is based on law. God planned the entire universe with very precise laws to guide every part of it, both very little things and very great. But everything we see around us—except human beings—obeys without choice. Men are not machines. We have free will. We have the gift of choice. We are invited to obey God's laws. And it is especially now, at this point in your lives, that the choice is offered to you in a new way. Life in Jesus is not for those who are lazy, indifferent, and selfish. But what would this invitation be without Jesus? Men have never lived together without laws. But no one has ever offered a better reason to live by law than Jesus—and that reason is love. There can be no real love without law; without law, love becomes mere sentimentality. But without love, law can become a fearful burden.

When he was asked which was the greatest commandment of God's law, Jesus said that love of God and neighbor sum up all the laws. We live by God's law, therefore, because we love God and each other. That makes all the difference.

You are being invited here to become closely united with Jesus. The rewards are great. Jesus is always challenging us, always expecting more from us—and always giving us the graces we need to meet his demands.

PART ONE

The Ten Commandments

CHAPTER 1

God Gives Us the Law

"And if you obey the voice of the LORD your God, being careful to do all his commandments which I command you this day, the LORD your God will set you high above all the nations of the earth."

Deuteronomy 28:1

If we observe the world around us, we will see that there is a certain order in the way things happen. Throw a stone in the air and it falls back to the ground. We say it does that because of the law of gravity. Wild geese will fly for miles and miles to return every year to the same place to nest and hatch their goslings. They do that by instinct. And if we look at men now and through the ages, in different countries and cultures, we find that they always have a rule about right and wrong: "Do good and avoid evil." Human beings all over the earth have the idea that they ought to behave in a certain way.

The difference between this rule of human behavior and the law of gravity or instinct is that the law of gravity or instinct tells us what things *do*, and the rule of human behavior tells us what we *ought* to do. In other words, the stone or goose has no choice in the matter. The stone doesn't decide to fall back to earth—it must. But while the rule of human behavior may tell us what is right and wrong to do, we are still free to decide just what we will do.

This presents two problems. The first problem is that though all men might agree that we should "do good and avoid evil," they don't always agree about what is good and

what is evil. In fact, people are often mistaken about what behavior is right and wrong. So how can we know for sure?

The second problem concerns our reasons for following this law of human behavior. Since men aren't forced to act in accord with law but may freely choose, why do they?

The Master Plan

Where can we find the solution to these problems? The best way is to look to the Master Planner and see what he had in mind.

As we all know, God is the Creator and Lord of heaven and earth. In his great wisdom he made the universe and governs it all. Now, just as he made the law of gravity and instinct, he made all men with this idea of doing good and avoiding evil. But he also made men with free will, allowing them to choose to do good and avoid evil.

When Adam and Eve chose to disobey God, their sin affected all men that were to come. One result of Original Sin is that it is harder for us to know what is right and wrong and to behave accordingly. If we read the beginning of the Old Testament we can easily see that men soon made a mess of things.

13

But God promised Adam that he would not abandon us and would give us a means of salvation. So God called upon Abraham and made him the father of his chosen people. God established his covenant with the Israelites, to show that he would be their God and they would be his people. He gave them the **Decalogue**—the **Ten Commandments**. God wanted his people to know what was right and wrong and what was truly good and truly bad for them. He was preparing them for a special role in salvation history.

Some people think that God simply wanted obedience to a set of rules. What he really wanted is a faithful people. He gave his people a law to teach and guide them in every part of their lives. Further, he gave his people a law to prepare them for the coming of the Savior.

Fulfillment of the Law

When Jesus came to establish the New **Covenant**, he did not set aside the Ten Commandments, but completed them. He said: "Do not think that I have come to abolish the law and the prophets; I have come not to abolish them but to fulfill them" (Mt 5:17). Jesus teaches that the foundation of all law is love: to love God above all things, with one's whole mind and heart and soul, and to love one's neighbor as oneself. Jesus wants all men to turn their minds and hearts to God with love. Disobeying any of the Ten Commandments is a failure to love either God or our neighbor. This is because the Ten Commandments sum up our duties to God and our neighbor.

Conscience

How do we know that one action is right and another wrong? Along with free will God has given each man the ability to judge if something is right or wrong. This ability is called **conscience**. Our conscience is a very practical tool. It tells us what would be right or wrong behavior in a given situation. We are to obey our conscience, for God gave it to us so that we could live according to his law.

Every person is born with a conscience. Even a member of some primitive tribe that has never come into contact with civilization has the same law in his heart to do good and avoid evil. His tribe will probably have a code of what they think is right and wrong. He will be responsible before God for doing what he thinks is right and not doing what he thinks is wrong. In this way he can please God. But his code of behavior might differ somewhat from the Ten Commandments. Since he has had no contact with the commandments, he will not be held responsible for obeying them. Nonetheless, his conscience is faulty.

A conscience has to be taught—and taught correctly. We call this "forming" a conscience. The conscience of the primitive man, since it was not formed correctly, is called an incorrect conscience. Since he could do nothing about

that, he will not be held responsible for his incorrect conscience. On the other hand, all men who have access to the Word of God have a responsibility to form a correct conscience.

God has given us the means to form our consciences correctly. He has revealed truths about himself and given us the Ten Commandments. To live according to the will of God we must follow and obey the commandments. If we disregard or break God's law we sin. If we deliberately break a commandment in a serious matter, we commit a mortal sin and destroy charity, or the love of God, in our hearts. When we commit a mortal sin, we reject God by choosing to do something seriously contrary to God's will. If we do not repent of mortal sin, we cannot go to heaven and be happy with God forever. Of course, whether or not what we do is a mortal sin depends on whether we know that what we are doing is seriously wrong and we freely chose to do it anyway. And if we do commit a mortal sin, God will forgive us if we truly repent of our sin. He has given us the Sacrament of Penance to forgive our sins and to help us to grow closer to him.

But besides giving us the Law, he has given us reasons why we should want to follow it. First, God is the giver and author of that law, and since he is our Creator he knows what is best for us. Obeying God's law is necessary

---

The Ten Commandments

1. I am the Lord your God; you shall not have other gods before me.
2. You shall not take the name of the Lord your God in vain.
3. Remember to keep holy the Lord's Day.
4. Honor your father and mother.
5. You shall not kill.
6. You shall not commit adultery.
7. You shall not steal.
8. You shall not bear false witness against your neighbor.
9. You shall not covet your neighbor's wife.
10. You shall not covet your neighbor's goods.

for our eternal salvation. How could we live with God forever if we choose to reject his life and his friendship by serious sin?

But an even greater reason to obey God is that we know his great love for us. Jesus tells us: "If you love me, you will keep my commandments." (Jn 14:15) What better way do we have of showing our love for God than by doing what he asks of us?

God gave us his commandments and our conscience to help us know right from wrong.

He gave us the example of his Son Jesus Christ, who perfectly loved and obeyed the Father. At the same time, God gave us the power to keep his commandments. That power is the life of grace that comes from the Holy Spirit who lives within us.

Words to Know:
Decalogue   Ten Commandments
covenant   conscience

Q. 1   *What must we do to live according to the will of God?*
To live according to the will of God, we must believe the truths that he has revealed and with the help of his grace obey his commandments (CCC 1692).

Q. 2   *What are the commandments of God?*
The commandments of God are the Ten Commandments, the moral laws that God gave to Moses on Mount Sinai in the Old Testament, and which Jesus Christ perfected in the New Testament.

Q. 3   *What is the foundation of all our duties toward God and neighbor?*
The foundation of all our duties toward God and neighbor is charity, as Jesus Christ explained: the greatest and first commandment is the love of God, and the second is love of neighbor; upon these two commandments depends the whole law and the prophets. (CCC 2055).

Q. 4   *Why are we obliged to keep the commandments of God?*
We are obliged to keep the commandments of God because they sum up our basic duties toward God and our neighbor (CCC 2072).

Q. 5   *Does one who deliberately breaks a commandment of God in a serious matter sin gravely?*
One who deliberately breaks even one commandment of God in a serious matter sins gravely against God, and thus risks hell (CCC 1855, 2072).

CHAPTER 2

The First Commandment In Our Own Day

"I am the LORD your God, who brought you out of the land of Egypt, out of the house of bondage. You shall have no other gods before me."

Exodus 20:2–3

The First Commandment requires all men to recognize or acknowledge God as the one true God, Creator and Lord of all things, and to **worship** and **adore** him as our God. As creatures, we owe everything to God; we are completely dependent on him. By our reverence and worship we acknowledge our debt and gratitude to our Creator.

To give God loving worship we must believe in him and believe all that he has revealed to us. This means that we must learn more about God. If he has given us the means to do this, we have no excuse for being ignorant about God and his truths.

This commandment requires certain behavior from us, it also forbids us to act in any way contrary to what we owe God. It is wrong if we practice **superstition** or impiety. **Impiety** means being irreverent and disrespectful of God or sacred things. It is also wrong if we willfully doubt some truth about God or refuse to know what we should about God and our religion. There are times when some people are so willful that they publicly acknowledge their disbelief in or disagreement with the truths of the Faith. This is called **heresy**—the denying or disagreeing with one particular truth, or **apostasy**—deserting or leaving the true religion.

Strange Gods

We have read about people in ancient times who used to worship idols—false gods, things like golden calves. Remember when the Israelites worshipped the golden calf in the desert before God gave them the Ten Commandments? This is called **idolatry**. We don't run into too many people who worship golden calves, but many still place "strange gods" before God in their lives.

Not to have "strange gods" means that we are not to love anyone or anything as much as we love God. We are to worship and adore him—that is, give him the special love that is owed to him alone. This is a love that acknowledges his supreme position above all creation.

We must put nothing God has made before our love for him. No creature is to be adored—that is, worshipped with that special love which we owe to God alone. Our love for or attachment to things God has made is not wrong in itself. It is not wrong for a computer or a dog to have a place in our life. But these things must never compete with our love for God or with his plans for us. For example, if we love a computer so much that we steal one, then we have put it before God.

There is a story from the Bible which makes all this clear.

The Rich Young Man

A rich young man received an invitation from our Lord himself to give up his riches and become a follower of Jesus. Saint Mark tells us that Jesus looked at the young man and loved him, for the youth had always kept all of God's commandments and wanted to do even better. Jesus said to him: "You lack one thing; go, sell what you have, and give to the poor, and you will have treasure in heaven; and come, follow me" (Mk 10:21).

But the young man turned away sadly and left Jesus because, as the Bible says, he "had many possessions." He could not follow Jesus

because he loved creatures, or created goods, too much. They may not have been the same creatures we have—not radios or televisions or cars—but whatever they were, he would not give them up. He missed the chance to follow Jesus because creatures were competing in his heart with love for God.

There is danger in having many possessions because they may turn our hearts from God. Our love for such things must be a "detached" love, a love that is ready to let go of things when God asks it of us.

Due Worship

In ages before Christ, the Hebrew people offered public **sacrifice** by slaughtering a valuable animal, like a lamb, upon an altar to honor God, to acknowledge him as Creator of all, and especially to make up for their sins.

The sacrifice of the Hebrew people pleased God but it could never fully make up for sin. As we know, the sin of Adam had closed the gates of heaven. None of the many sacrifices offered by the Hebrews could change this. For sin offends God who is so great, and no offering of man alone, no matter how valuable, can make up for it.

Man's helplessness was no obstacle to God who wanted to save man. God himself became man and offered himself on the Cross as a fitting sacrifice, which was far more than enough to make up for all sins of all men. This sacrifice is renewed daily in every Mass around the world. The sacrifice of Jesus on the Cross is the greatest gift we can offer to God.

The sacrifice we offer in the Mass is the highest possible act of worship. It contains all that is necessary for giving due worship to God. In the Mass we acknowledge God as Creator, our Lord and Master. We thank him in gratitude for all he has given us. And, in recognition that we are dependent on him, we ask for all we need and for what will help others. Finally, we offer in the Mass the only thing that can make up for our sins and offenses. We offer the sacrifice of Jesus Christ on the Cross.

We can give God the love and worship we owe him when we participate in Holy Mass. Let's do so often!

Words to Know:

worship adore superstition impiety
heresy idolatry sacrifice apostasy

"Bless the Lord, all works of the Lord, sing praise to him and highly exalt him for ever."

Daniel 3:35

19

Q. 6   *What are we required to do by the First Commandment?*
The First Commandment commands us to believe in God, to hope in him, and to love him above all else (CCC 2134).

Q. 7   *What does the First Commandment forbid?*
The First Commandment forbids heresy, apostasy, voluntary doubt, deliberate ignorance of God's truth, despair, presumption, idolatry, indifference to God, hatred of God, superstition, and irreligious behavior (CCC 2110).

Q. 8   *How does the story of the rich young man teach us to avoid putting possessions above God?*
The story of the rich young man showed that he was overly attached to his many possessions and therefore did not follow Jesus. This is an example of how many people, even today, commit idolatry (CCC 2113).

Q. 9   *How did the Hebrews offer worship to God?*
The Hebrews offered worship to God through animal sacrifice (CCC 1539).

Q. 10   *What was the perfect sacrifice made to God?*
The perfect sacrifice made to God was the offering of Jesus Christ upon the Cross, which was the perfect act of worship (CCC 2100).

Q. 11   *How can we participate in Jesus' perfect act of worship due to God?*
We can participate in Jesus' perfect act of worship due to God by participating in the Mass, since the Sacrifice of the Mass and the Sacrifice of the Cross are one and the same sacrifice (CCC 1369, 2100).

CHAPTER 3

Prayer–Hidden Treasure

"Lord, teach us to pray, as John taught his disciples."

Luke 11:1

> The chief exercise of prayer is to speak to God and to hear God speak in the depths of your heart.
>
> —Saint Francis de Sales

Prayer is something required of us by the First Commandment. It is necessary for us to pray, and we must do so every day. God commanded us to pray, and he listens to our prayers.

Prayer is defined as the raising of the mind and heart to God. Our prayer is our conversation with God. It may be done briefly or at length. We must have God in mind when we pray. We must think of something about him which moves us to love him. Then we can talk with him, adore him, tell him we are sorry for our sin, ask him for things we need, and listen to him, too. One of the best ways to do this is to consider something Jesus said or did. Jesus, being man as well as God, can be pictured in the imagination. This helps to stir our heart, and then we can, for instance, make an act of faith, an act of hope, or an act of love.

Three forms of prayer are vocal prayer, meditation, and contemplation. In vocal prayer, we use our voice to express a set prayer (such as the Our Father) or a personal prayer. In meditation we use our mind, heart, and imagi-nation to consider and seek the Lord and his will for us. Often meditation uses books, such as the Bible, to seek the Lord. In contempla-tive prayer, we are simply and lovingly united to God.

Our Need to Pray

Jesus strongly encourages us to pray. Saint Luke records, "And he [Jesus] told them a par-able, to the effect that they ought always to pray and not lose heart" (Lk 18:1).

This means that we must pray even when we do not feel like it, as well as when we do. We must pray when unwanted thoughts inter-rupt our concentration or when worries tug us away from our thoughts about God, about Jesus, and about the saints. These interrup-tions are called "distractions." When they hap-pen, we must return to prayer calmly and patiently. Distractions like these are not our fault. But if we begin to daydream and, after we realize it, continue to daydream instead of pray, we are at fault. If my mind wanders a hundred times, and I direct it back to prayer each time, there is no fault. In fact, there is great merit because this is hard work and shows God that I love him and want to please him. By praying to God—asking for what we need, thanking him for what he has given us—we acknowledge that we are his creatures and that we are totally dependent on him.

"Let my prayer be counted as incense before you, and the lifting up of my hands as an evening sacrifice."

Psalm 141:2

Jesus assures us that our prayers will be answered. He says: "Ask, and it will be given you; seek, and you will find; knock, and it will be opened to you" (Mt 7:7).

We will not, of course, get what is bad for us or what is really unnecessary. But God will always give us what is best for us.

Particular Prayers

There is a special prayer of the Church called the Liturgy of the Hours or the **Divine Office**. The Divine Office is a prayer of praise and petition using the Psalms and readings from Scripture and the writings of the saints. Certain members of the Church, such as priests, are required to pray the Divine Office every day, but all of us in the Church are invited to join in the Church's praise of God in this rich and beautiful form of prayer.

Another prayer especially recommended by the Church is the Rosary. For about eight hundred years, countless numbers of the faithful have made it part of their daily prayer. The Rosary is divided into mysteries, episodes in the lives of Jesus and Mary. We are to think about these mysteries as we say the vocal prayers—mainly the Hail Marys. The prayers should be said slowly as our hearts are moved by what is in our minds. And what could be better suited to help us pray than scenes from the lives of Jesus and Mary?

* * *

A life of prayer is sometimes called the spiritual life or the devout life. Our spiritual life is the sum of all we do to reach heaven, which includes receiving the Sacraments and doing good works. The spiritual life is a way of growing; and the more we grow in prayer, the more joy, peace, and confidence we will have. A life of prayer makes us fully alive!

Jesus said: "These things I have spoken to you, that my joy may be in you, and that your joy may be full" (Jn 15:11).

Words to Know:
prayer   Divine Office (Liturgy of the Hours)

Form the habit of speaking to God as if you were alone with him, familiarly and with confidence and love, as to the dearest and most loving of friends. Speak to him often of your business, your plans, your troubles, your fears— of everything that concerns you. Talk with him confidently and frankly; for God does not often speak to a soul that does not speak to him.

—Saint Alphonsus Liguori

Q. 12   *What is prayer?*
Prayer is the lifting of the mind and heart to God, in order to know him better, to adore him, to thank him, and to ask him for what we need (CCC 2590).

Q. 13   *What kinds of prayer are there?*
There are five kinds of prayer: blessing and adoration, prayer of petition, prayer of intercession, prayer of thanksgiving, and prayer of praise (CCC 2626–49).

Q. 14   *What is mental prayer?*
Mental prayer is that which is said with the mind and heart alone (CCC 2708).

Q. 15   *What is vocal prayer?*

Vocal prayer is that which is expressed by spoken words with the participation of the mind and heart (CCC 2700).

Q. 16   *How should we pray?*

We should pray humbly, attentively, and devoutly (CCC 2559).

Q. 17   *Why is it necessary to pray?*

It is necessary to pray in order to grow in our faith in God, in our hope in him, and in our love for him, and in this way to receive the grace necessary to be united with him in heaven (CCC 2558).

Q. 18   *How should we pray, and what for?*

We should give glory, thanksgiving, and praise to God in our daily prayer. We should hallow (make holy) his name. We should ask for whatever is necessary to obtain eternal life, including things necessary for life in this world. We should ask forgiveness for our sins. Jesus Christ taught us to do this in the Our Father (CCC 2857).

Q. 19   *What is the most perfect prayer?*

The Mass is the most perfect prayer because in it Jesus offers himself to the Father for us. We offer ourselves along with Jesus to the Father by the power of the Holy Spirit (CCC 1358–59, 1369, 1407).

Saints—They Made The Most of It

"After this I looked, and behold, a great multitude which no man could number, from every nation, from all tribes and peoples and tongues, standing before the throne and before the Lamb, clothed in white robes, with palm branches in their hands."

Revelation 7:9

In this life we are all looking for the same thing: *happiness*. **Saints** are those who have found it. They are perfectly happy with God in heaven. On earth they enjoyed a special closeness to God that brought them great happiness even in the midst of their sufferings. But there is one thing we must always remember about the saints: they all started out just like each of us. What is more, each of us is called to be a saint, too.

Many a saint, writing or speaking about his life, remembered being unhappy for years while he ignored God and followed the ways of the world. He might have forgotten his unhappiness for awhile in seeking pleasure, but when the pleasure ended he was sadder than before. Then he had a change of heart, turned to God, and began a new life. This new beginning in God is called a conversion. Through prayer and the Sacraments he practiced loving God, and he practiced loving his neighbors by doing good works. His old life of sin was over and his new life with Christ gave him joy.

The great Saint Augustine wrote: "You have made us for yourself, O Lord, and our hearts are restless until they rest in you."

We can only be happy if we are in harmony with the will of God, which means we are doing what God wants. Any distance from God, great or small, caused by sin, means that much unhappiness. The key to happiness, then, is "friendship with God," which means doing God's will. The saints are close friends of God. This friendship brings them great joy, for we were made for friendship with God and nothing else can make up for that if we do not have it.

There is only one cure for the unhappy man: he must turn to God with all his heart. Nothing else can satisfy him.

Jesus relates **sanctity**, or happiness and holiness, to the "Kingdom of God." He compares true happiness to a merchant's search for fine pearls: "The kingdom of heaven is like a merchant in search of fine pearls, who, on finding one pearl of great value, went and sold all that he had and bought it" (Mt 13:45–46).

Saint Charles Lwanga

Saint John Bosco

Saint Maximilian Kolbe

"To the saints honor must be paid as friends of Christ, as sons and heirs of God."

—Saint John of Damascus

This is what the saints have done. In many cases they have completely changed their lives in order to obey God and be at peace with him. Now, after a happy life on earth, they enjoy the full and tremendous happiness of seeing God in heaven.

Saints Victorious

We call the saints in heaven the **Church Triumphant** because they have grasped the final prize which is God himself. God has given himself to them; he is theirs for all eternity. "Eternal life" doesn't just mean living forever; it means living *God's* life forever.

Intercessors

We should take advantage of the great power of the saints to intercede for us. "Intercede" means to speak up for someone, to pray for someone. We should pray to the saints and ask them to do this. They are called "**intercessors**"— those who intercede. When we pray to the saints we are honoring them, and in honoring them we honor God because we acknowledge that through God's grace they have been victo-

rious over sin. We ask other people on earth to pray to God for us. We can also ask the saints in heaven to intercede for us. Their prayers are very powerful because they are dear friends of God. Each of us should pray, particularly, to his **patron saint**, the saint for whom he was named. We should pray especially to the Blessed Virgin Mary, who is the greatest of all the saints, given to us as our Mother by Jesus himself. We have many special prayers to Mary, but the best known is the "Hail Mary." We should also pray to the good angels, although we know the names of only three of them: Saint Michael the Archangel, Saint Gabriel, whom God sent to the Blessed Virgin to ask her to become the Mother of his Son, and Saint Raphael. We should pray every day to our own guardian angel, for he is always with us to help us. In addition, we should pray to our favorite saints, those for whom we feel a special attraction.

Besides asking the saints to intercede for us, we should study their lives so that we may learn from them how to attain our goal of heaven. By imitating their virtuous lives we will find it easier to know and fulfill the will of God.

We should keep in mind that the saints are real people who are now with Jesus in heaven. If we make friends with them today, they will remember us when we need them most. They will help us grow closer to Jesus.

The Blessed in Heaven

Those whom we honor by name as saints are those whom the Church has determined with complete certainty to be now in heaven. There are many, many others in heaven unknown to us whom we will meet when we get there.

How many saints are there, including all those of whom we do not now know?

Saint John, in the Book of Revelation, tells us of a vision of heaven: "After this I looked, and behold, a great multitude which no man could number, from every nation, from all tribes and peoples and tongues" (Rev 7:9).

This is comforting, but we should never take heaven for granted. With Saint Paul we must "finish the race;" we must "fight the good fight" (see 2 Tim 4:7). We must follow Jesus in order to be with him one day in heaven; the saints can help us do this.

Words to Know:

saints   sanctity   Church Triumphant intercessor   patron saint

Q. 15 *Who are the saints?*

The saints are those who, by practicing the virtues to a heroic degree according to the teachings and example of Jesus Christ, have merited special glory in heaven and also on earth, where, by the authority of the Church, they are publicly honored and called upon (CCC 828, 927).

Q. 16 *Why should we pray to the saints in addition to God?*

We should pray to the saints in addition to God because God wills to help us through the prayers of others, including the saints, who are very holy and close to God (CCC 956).

Q. 17 *Why are the angels, the saints, and our Lady powerful intercessors with God?*

The angels and saints are powerful intercessors with God because they are his faithful servants and his beloved friends. Our Lady is the most powerful intercessor of all because she is the Mother of God. She is also a model for all who pray (CCC 956, 2679).

Q. 18 *What is the prayer that we use in a special way to invoke the intercession of our Lady?*

We invoke the intercession of our Lady especially with the Hail Mary (CCC 2676–77).

CHAPTER 5

The Holy Name

"You shall not take the name of the LORD your God in vain; for the LORD will not hold him guiltless who takes his name in vain."

Exodus 20:7

The Second Commandment forbids any lack of respect, or due **reverence**, toward God in the use of his most Holy Name, or toward any holy person or thing. Anyone who offends God by breaking this commandment is usually spiritually unwell, since no one who truly loves God would think of purposely misusing his name. On the contrary, someone who loves God goes out of his way to bless God's name and to make up for the times when others misuse his name.

When Moses asked God for his name, God said, "I AM WHO I AM." (Ex 3:14) For the Jewish people this name was so great and holy because it was the name that God personally revealed out of love.

What terrible foolishness, therefore, to misuse so great a Name!

* * *

There are different ways in which people violate the Second Commandment.

One way is called **blasphemy**. This is verbal abuse or scorn toward God himself or, by extension, toward the Blessed Virgin, the other saints, or holy things.

Another violation is swearing false oaths. A false **oath** calls on God to witness to the truth of what we are saying when in fact we are lying. An oath in itself is not wrong. We may be involved in a legal proceeding which requires one. This is a good enough reason to take an oath; however, we should not take oaths invoking the divine name without serious reason.

Obviously, a false oath is a very serious sin, since we are calling God, who is all Truth and all Justice, to witness to a lie.

Aside from the formality of a legal proceeding, it is common for people to use expressions like, "As God is my witness," or, "Honest to God." Spoken seriously, these are oaths and should not be used lightly. Said thoughtlessly or for unimportant reasons, they are swearing and should be avoided. (We must not confuse swearing with using bad language or cursing; using impure language is against the Sixth Commandment and cursing against the Fifth.)

The Second Commandment also requires us to fulfill the vows and promises we have made. A vow is a solemn declaration committing oneself to do something. A **vow** in religion is a vow by which someone promises something for a religious reason. Religious brothers and sisters make vows of poverty, chastity, and obedience. A married couple makes a vow of fidelity.

Holy Things

We must not only respect God but must extend that respect to all those things that belong to God in a special way. We refer to our church as the house of God and a place of worship. It is a building consecrated to the glorification of God, and our behavior in church ought to express that.

All of the objects used for Mass, such as the altar, chalice, and paten, are holy because they are used in the highest form of worship. It is easy to see why we revere the Holy Bible, since it is the Word of God. Just as we treasure pictures and mementos of those we love, we also cherish crucifixes, religious medals, and holy images as reminders of God and his saints.

Certain people within the Church (the Pope, bishops, priests, deacons, religious brothers and sisters) have consecrated their entire lives to God. Because they belong to God in a special way, we honor and respect them.

We express our love and reverence for God in the way we treat those things and people that belong to God.

Remember what God said to Moses from the burning bush: "Moses, Moses! . . . Do not come near; put off your shoes from your feet, for the place on which you are standing is holy ground" (Ex 3:4–5). The ground was holy because God was present.

Words to Know:
> reverence   blasphemy
> oath   vow

Holy Name Society

Some parishes have an organization called the Holy Name Society. This society goes back to the thirteenth century. Its aim is to bring about due love and reverence for the Holy Name of God and Jesus Christ.

"O LORD, our Lord, how majestic is your name in all the earth!"

Psalm 8:1

"From the rising of the sun to its setting the name of the LORD is to be praised!"

Psalm 113:3

"Young men and maidens together, old men and children! Let them praise the name of the LORD, for his name alone is exalted."

Psalm 148:12–13

Q. 19 *What does the Second Commandment require us to do?*
The Second Commandment requires us to respect and revere the Holy Name of God and to fulfill the vows and promises to which we have bound ourselves (CCC 2142, 2150).

Q. 20 *What does the Second Commandment forbid?*
The Second Commandment forbids us from dishonoring the name of God. To dishonor the name of God means to use his name without respect; to blaspheme God, the Holy Virgin, the saints, or holy things; or to swear oaths that are false, unnecessary, or wrong in any way (CCC 2146–49).

Q. 21 *What is an oath?*
An oath is calling upon God as witness for what is declared or promised. A person who swears falsely offends God seriously, for God is holiness and truth itself (CCC 2149–50).

Q. 22 *Is blasphemy a serious sin?*
Yes, blasphemy is a serious sin because it is injury and scorn toward God and his saints (CCC 2148).

Q. 23 *What is a vow?*
A vow is a promise made to God of some good that is pleasing to him (CCC 2102).

HALLOWED BE THY NAME

CHAPTER 6

The Lord's Day

"Remember the sabbath day, to keep it holy."

Exodus 20:8

Time is precious. Most people would agree on that. But this does not mean the same thing to everyone. Most people think that they never have enough time to do what *they* want to do.

So when God asks for some of our time for himself, people react differently. Some are so happy to give time to God that they are grateful for every opportunity. Others can't be bothered. They are shortsighted, for all men eventually run out of time, while God alone possesses a world without end which he wants to share with us. As we say in the prayer:

> Glory be to the Father and to the Son and to the Holy Spirit; as it was in the beginning, is now, and ever shall be, *world without end. Amen.*

The Third Commandment tells us to give one day a week to God. It is written: "Six days you shall labor, and do all your work; but the seventh day is a sabbath to the LORD your God" (Ex 20:9–10). The **Sabbath** is a *holy* day, which, like anything holy, is consecrated or dedicated to God, set aside for him. God himself says that in six days he made the world and on the seventh he rested.

The Jewish people observe the Sabbath on Saturday, the last day of the week and the day on which God rested. But Christians observe Sunday instead, the day Jesus Christ, our Savior, rose from the dead. We give him this day, this entire day, to show that we recognize who he is and to honor and glorify him. Each Sunday is like Easter; we are celebrating the Resurrection of the Lord and his triumph over death.

Making Sunday a Holy Day

We owe God a double debt as Creator and Redeemer, and we make some repayment—at least a small amount—by making Sunday a really holy day.

First of all, we put aside our work, which has had our attention all week long, and we turn our eyes to God, because although work is very good and necessary, it is nevertheless a concern with what God has made—creation—and not with God who made it.

For this reason we are commanded not to do any unnecessary work on Sundays and Holy Days. Our jobs and unnecessary school-work should be set aside. There are some jobs which make it necessary for some people to work on Sunday, such as doctors and nurses, policemen, bus drivers, farmers, and others who must work because of economic necessity;

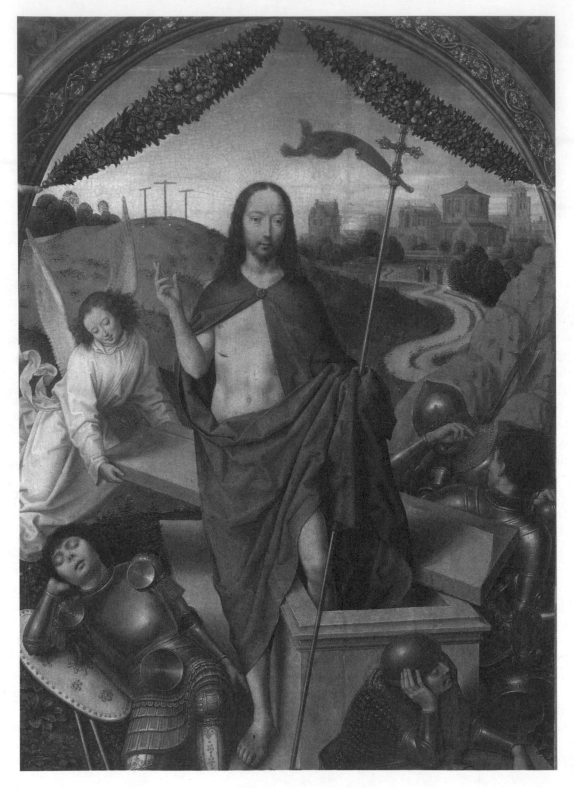

but most jobs can and should be put aside on Sunday.

The Third Commandment demands of us some form of external worship, not just internal or private worship. This is because our entire being is subject to God, both body and soul. We need to demonstrate this external worship publicly as a witness to the whole community that God has first place in our lives. God desires that our devotion be visible; he wants to be worshipped in broad daylight for all the world to see. Private devotion cannot take the place of this. If we omit outward worship together as a community, our faith will weaken and we may fall away from God.

The main way we worship God on the Lord's Day is by taking part in the Holy Sacrifice of the Mass because it is the greatest act of worship. For a Catholic, Sunday without Holy Mass is not a holy day. To miss Mass on Sunday is a mortal sin—unless, of course, there is a serious reason, such as sickness.

Mass on Sunday is an obligation we are bound to, but it is also a blessed opportunity for us. Anyone making a sincere effort to live the gospel will go not only to Holy Mass but to Holy Communion, as well, if he is prepared and worthy. Not to go to Sunday Mass is to cut ourselves off from the Sacraments and the grace which flows through them from Jesus to us. For Jesus says: "I am the vine, you are the branches. He who abides in me, and I in him, he it is that bears much fruit, for apart from me you can do nothing" (Jn 15:5).

Missing Mass on Sunday without a good reason is seriously wrong. It is also a great pity to go to Mass regularly but stay away from the Sacraments of Penance and Holy Communion. This would be a sign that Sunday Mass is just a duty, that there is no life in our observance, and that we do not understand much about the life of the Spirit or taste much of the goodness of the Lord.

* * *

There is great disrespect for the Lord's Day in our society, and it is growing all the time. It has always been understood that certain stores and certain services, such as hospitals and the police, have to be available on Sunday. Now we see people buying all sorts of unnecessary things in department stores that hum with business on this day, as if it were a day like any other. It is a sign that many people have lost touch with the spiritual side of life. We would not have such abuses of the Lord's Day if people realized that Sunday is a time to become like Jesus.

Day of Rest

Besides being a day to attend Mass, Sunday is supposed to be a day of joy and refreshment. Wholesome fun is a wonderful ingredient of holiness. We may take time for reading good books, more personal prayer and private devotions, works of charity, sports, hobbies, and real rest.

Let's use our imagination! As Mother Teresa of Calcutta said, let's do "something beautiful for God!" Let's really make Sunday a holy day.

"This is the day which the LORD has made; let us rejoice and be glad in it."

Psalm 118:24

Holy Days of Obligation

In addition to the obligation of Sunday Mass, there are **Holy Days of Obligation**, days which have the same obligation as Sundays.

The universal Church has ten Holy Days of Obligation. In certain countries attendance at Mass is not obligatory on all these Holy Days.

In the United States some of these are celebrated on Sunday and only six are considered Holy Days of Obligation. These six are the Solemnity of Mary Mother of God, Ascension, the Assumption of Mary, All Saints' Day, the Immaculate Conception of Mary, and Christmas.

- January 1, the Solemnity of Mary, Mother of God
- The Solemnity of the Ascension, forty days after Easter
- August 15, the Solemnity of the Assumption of the Blessed Virgin Mary
- November 1, the Solemnity of All Saints
- December 8, the Solemnity of the Immaculate Conception
- December 25, the Solemnity of the Nativity of Our Lord Jesus Christ

Words to Know:
Sabbath   Holy Days of Obligation

Q. 24 *What does the Third Commandment require us to do?*

The Third Commandment requires us to honor God on Sundays and Holy Days by acts of public worship. We do this most perfectly by taking part in Holy Mass (CCC 2180).

Q. 25 *Why must we do acts of external worship?*

It is not sufficient to adore God internally in the heart. We must also give him external worship because we are subject to God in our entire being—body and soul. We are also bound to give good examples. If we were to omit external worship we might lose our religious spirit.

Q. 26 *Are we required to take part in Mass?*

We are required to take part in Mass on Sunday and on the Holy Days of Obligation (CCC 2180).

Q. 27 *What does the Third Commandment forbid?*

The Third Commandment forbids unnecessary work or other activity that hinders worship of God and proper relaxation of the mind and body on Sunday and other Holy Days (CCC 2185).

Q. 28 *Which days are the Holy Days of Obligation?*

In the United States, the Holy Days of Obligation include the Solemnity of Mary, Mother of God, the Ascension, the Assumption of Mary, All Saints Day, the Immaculate Conception of Mary, and Christmas (CCC 2042, 2177).

Q. 29 *Why do Christians worship on Sunday?*

Christians worship on Sunday, the first day of the week, because Jesus rose from the dead on Easter Sunday (CCC 2169, 2174).

CHAPTER 7

The Cross and True Riches

"Then Jesus told his disciples, 'If any man would come after me, let him deny himself and take up his cross and follow me.'"

Matthew 16:24

The path through life to heaven is often compared to climbing a mountain, and the mountain-top is heaven, God's holy mountain. In Psalm 43, the pilgrim on life's journey cries out to God:

> Oh, send out your light and your truth;
> let them lead me,
> let them bring me to your holy hill,
> and to your dwelling! (Ps 43:3)

Christ our Savior offers us a way that will lead to peace, joy, and our final goal of total happiness with God. The way that leads to this wonderful state of perfection, or holiness, is based on Jesus' words: "If any man would come after me, let him deny himself and take up his cross daily and follow me" (Lk 9:23).

Self-denial means doing something we would rather not do or refusing some pleasure we would like for the sake of some greater good, for example, taking time to help your brother with his fractions or giving up dessert sometimes. Another example is giving your schoolwork your best effort, although it may not be easy and you may have to give up much of your free time to do it. Your schoolwork (or perhaps a particular subject) may take on the nature of a cross, especially if it is difficult.

Now we have come to a great mystery—the doctrine of the Cross. It is the principal sign of Christianity. As a result of Original Sin, it is necessary for us to put to death in ourselves a certain way of living which Saint Paul calls "the old man" and to put on "the new man," Jesus.

The old man is Adam, who misused the gifts of God and so brought sin and disorder into the world. As you know, this sin is passed on to all of us as Adam's children. We are born in the state of Original Sin. Through Baptism, Original Sin is washed away and we are given the life of grace. However, Original Sin has left in us many wounds and disorders. These wounds can only be healed by God's grace through a lifetime of right living, prayer, and self-denial.

This is not always easy. When Jesus asks us to love our enemy and to do good to those who hurt us, he is not asking us to do something that comes naturally or easily. But, by the power of God, it is not impossible. For with God "all things are possible" (Mt 19:26).

Our daily cross is all the things which, naturally speaking, we dislike. Our cross may be a penance we choose for ourselves or suffering that God allows in our life—perhaps an enemy at school or some sickness. Such sufferings are permitted for our good or the good of others,

"God loves a cheerful giver."
2 Corinthians 9:7

though we may not be able to see it at the time.

Bearing the crosses (that is, trials and difficulties) which we do not choose but which come to us anyhow in the course of life is a most perfect kind of self-denial, more pleasing to God than the acts of self-denial we choose for ourselves. For in all things it is most perfect to accept the will of God, even when we do not like it very much. Jesus' entire life was one of obedience to the will of the Father, no matter how hard it was or what it required of him, even his death. "Father, if you are willing, remove this chalice from me; nevertheless not my will, but yours, be done" (Lk 22:42).

And why are we willing to set out on such a way of life? In following the example of Jesus we are showing our love for God by willingly and, yes, even cheerfully accepting whatever he permits.

Fast and Abstinence

We are encouraged to choose some **penance** for ourselves. To help us, the Church requires **fasting** and **abstinence** from certain foods on penitential days. To abstain, in this case, means not to eat meat. If we are fourteen years old or more, we must abstain from meat on Ash Wednesday and Good Friday.

In the United States, the bishops have declared abstinence from meat on all Fridays of Lent. In other seasons, Friday remains a day of penance on which we are supposed to practice some kind of self-denial, and the Church advises us to make Friday a day of abstinence all year round.

Fasting, in general, means not eating at all. When the Church requires us to fast, however, it means that only one full meal a day should be eaten. In addition, two smaller meals may be taken, but those taken together should not equal another full meal. In the Church, there are two days of required fasting: Ash Wednesday and Good Friday. This applies to anyone eighteen to sixty years old.

Penitential Seasons

Advent and **Lent** are special seasons in the Church year in which we are reminded to renew our spirit. They are called penitential seasons.

Advent begins four Sundays before Christmas and is a season of special preparation for celebrating the birth of Christ. The Church suggests that we do some form of penance as part of this preparation.

The season of Lent begins six and a half weeks before Easter and is a season of preparation for the Passion, death, and Resurrection

"And when you fast, do not look dismal, like the hypocrites, for they disfigure their faces that their fasting may be seen by men. Truly, I say to you, they have received their reward. But when you fast, anoint your head and wash your face, that your fasting may not be seen by men but by your Father who is in secret; and your Father who sees in secret will reward you."

(Matthew 6:16–18)

of the Lord. Just as Jesus fasted for forty days, we too take on some penance during Lent to make up for our sins and to prepare our hearts to celebrate the great Easter feast.

Saint Paul compares the spiritual life to a race and the Christian to an athlete. Like an athlete, the Christian is asked to practice certain spiritual exercises. If an athlete will give up a great deal just to train for a race, how much more should we Christians be ready to practice self-denial for the sake of the Kingdom of God!

Besides, what the athlete gives up in training is not always so great, and his self-discipline is often very satisfying, invigorating, and enjoyable. His muscle tone, increased skill, and sense of well-being make it all worthwhile.

It is the same way with the Kingdom of God. The crosses we bear can include the many little things which make up our daily lives, such as not always having our own way, forgiving an unkind word, turning from fun to duties at the proper time, not overeating, and the like. We are not expected to make life one big penance with no pleasures. After all, it is God who created the things in which we find pleasure. But, like a good athlete, we must keep an eye on the coach— Jesus—and not forget ourselves and break training.

By God's grace, penance can make up for past sin and help prevent future sin. It helps eliminate those things that take us away from God or are obstacles to our final goal—union with God in his Kingdom.

Words to Know:

self-denial   penance   fasting
abstinence   Advent   Lent

Rules of Fast and Abstinence in the United States

— The days and times of penance for the universal Church are each Friday of the whole year and the whole season of Lent.
— Abstinence and fasting are to be observed on Ash Wednesday and Good Friday. Abstinence is to be observed on all the Fridays during Lent.
— The law of abstinence binds those who have completed their fourteenth year. The law of fasting binds those eighteen years old to sixty years old.

Dearest Lord, teach me to be generous;
teach me to serve you as you deserve to be served—
to give and not to count the cost,
to fight and not to heed the wounds,
to toil and not to seek for rest,
to labor and not to ask any reward
except that of knowing that I do your holy will.

—Saint Ignatius Loyola

Q. 30 *What is abstinence?*

To abstain from something is to give it up voluntarily. A day of abstinence in the Church is one during which we abstain from eating meat (CIC, Canon 1251).

Q. 31 *What is penance?*

Penance is an act of self-denial or prayer that helps strengthen us to do God's will and, by his grace, to make up for sin (CCC 1434, 2043).

Q. 32 *When are the days and times for penance for the universal Church?*

All Fridays of the year and the time of Lent are days and times of penance for the universal Church (CCC 1438).

Q. 33 *What are the days when both fasting and abstinence are required in the universal Church?*

The days when both fasting and abstinence are required in the universal Church are Ash Wednesday and Good Friday (CIC, Canon 1251).

Q. 34 *In the United States what other days are days of required abstinence?*

Other days of required abstinence in the United States are all Fridays during Lent (CCC 1438).

CHAPTER 8

In the Heart of the Family

"Honor your father and your mother, that your days may be long in the land which the LORD your God gives you."

Exodus 20:12

We sometimes see elderly people with their children who are themselves approaching old age. No matter how old the parents are, no matter how old the children, the law of the Lord remains: "Honor your father and your mother."

Even without the Fourth Commandment we would be able to see that we have certain obligations toward our parents, for we would never have existed without them. They are special; they have given us life. This gift is so great that there is no way to repay them completely.

To see what is required of us by the Fourth Commandment, we need to look at family relations. Without children, husband and wife make a marriage; with a child, they make a family. The child is an extension of their love for each other and is included in their love. The relation of parent to child is a lasting one, no matter how old one is. It is from his parents that a child learns what love is. In that love the child is able to learn that God is also his loving Father.

Each child is a precious gift from God. But along with the blessing of a child there are many duties and responsibilities that parents must take on. God gives them the authority and duty to maintain good order in the home, to provide food and clothing, to educate, and to tend to the welfare of each of their children.

Now, the commandment tells us to **honor** our parents. To honor means to hold in high regard, to respect, and to love. A child honors his parents when he respects their authority over him. This also includes respecting and obeying government authorities, clergy, and those whom our parents place in authority over us, such as a teacher or scout leader.

God provides for the well-being and development of children by placing them under the loving authority of their parents, and so obedience to that authority is required.

With the years, children may discover faults and weaknesses in their parents, but they must still honor them. Children can sometimes be a powerful force for good and a source of grace for their parents. Prayer and sacrifice for the welfare of one's parents are always blessed by God.

As children get older they need less care and direction until they reach a point at which they are able to order their own lives. It is only reasonable, then, that the relationship between parent and child should gradually change. Obedience turns into respect for the wisdom of

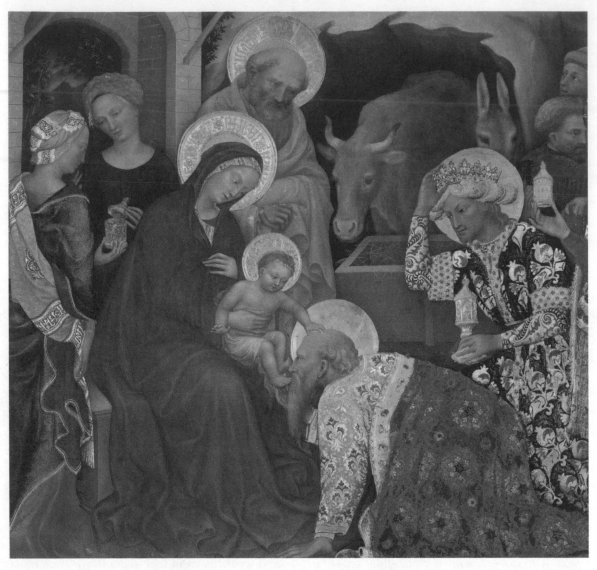

our parents until we reach an age at which we are no longer bound by obedience but still gratefully accept our parents' advice.

Anyone who honors his parents will, when he grows older, look after their needs. In this regard, life is like a seesaw with the heavier end holding up the other. As a youngster, the child sits at the end upraised, with mother and father holding down the other. Many years later, the child holds the seesaw down while the elderly parents receive the care and attention. They cared for us; now we care for them.

The Bible teaches: "O son, help your father in his old age, and do not grieve him as long as he lives" (Sir 3:12).

And God promises to bless those who keep the Fourth Commandment:

"Honor your father and your mother, that your days may be long in the land which the LORD your God gives you" (Ex 20:12).

The Family Today

In his Apostolic Exhortation *Familiaris Consortio*, "The Role of the Christian Family in the Modern World," Saint John Paul II singled out the family as the main means for the renewal of modern society. The family is so important that we cannot hope to survive as a society unless family life is healthy and strong. This means that strong love among all the members must unite the whole family and make it holy.

The Holy Family, Jesus, Mary, and Joseph, was united with that holy love. We should look to them as our model for family life.

There are many forces in our society that weaken the bonds of family life and even threaten to destroy it. The Christian family will survive only with renewed love for God and neighbor. We must pray together for our own families and for the family in general. Where there is no prayer, there will be no family unity and no peace. With prayer, we can hope for the blessings of family happiness on earth and reunion in our heavenly home.

Word to Know:

honor

Q. 35   *What does the Fourth Commandment require us to do?*
The Fourth Commandment commands us to love, respect, and obey our parents and others who have authority over us (CCC 2199).

Q. 36   *What does the Fourth Commandment forbid?*
The Fourth Commandment forbids us to disobey our parents and others in legitimate authority over us (CCC 2197).

Father, it is your commandment that we should honor our father and mother; hear the prayers I offer you for my parents. Grant them many years on earth, and keep them healthy in mind and body. Bless their work and all they do. Give them back a hundredfold whatever they have done for me. Inspire them with your love, and help them to fulfill your holy law. One day, may I be their comfort and support, so that, having enjoyed their affection on earth, I may have the joy of being with them forever in your home in heaven. Through Christ our Lord. *Amen.*

CHAPTER 9

Citizenship–
Rights and Duties

"So then you are no longer strangers and sojourners, but you are fellow citizens with the saints and members of the household of God."

Ephesians 2:19

As members of a family, we depend on others and they depend on us. This dependence of people on each other exists in society too. We are members of a state as well as a family. A state is a society of people united under a common government or authority. Our parents exercise a certain rightful authority over us, and so does the state. It is part of human nature for men to live together and to form societies with governments that exercise authority. Like our parents' authority, the state's authority comes from God. Saint Paul tells us: "Let every person be subject to the governing authorities. For there is no authority except from God. . . . Therefore he who resists the authorities resists what God has appointed" (Rom 13:1–2).

The state has the authority to make just laws for its citizens. The purpose of the state is to promote what is truly good for all members of its society. We call this the common good. The common good includes all the things in a society that allow people as individuals or in groups to have what they need in order to be truly happy. Jesus never denied the role of the government. When he was asked if people should pay taxes to the emperor Caesar, Jesus

said, "Render therefore to Caesar the things that are Caesar's, and to God the things that are God's" (Mt 22:21). In this way, Jesus taught that we have things we owe to God and things we owe to the state (Caesar).

The state should never demand something of us that is against God's law. If it does, it is denying its own authority, since that authority comes from God. The state is supposed to use its authority as God intends. This use of authority includes respecting God's law, encouraging virtue, and allowing people to be free to live according to that law.

As you probably already know, there are different kinds of government. God has never told us that one particular type of government is better than another. There can be several legitimate and good ways to govern a nation. The important thing is that the government respects and promotes the rights and well-being of all the people for the sake of the common good.

Good Citizens

Just as the state has certain rights and duties, so do we as citizens. As Christians we must be good citizens, obeying all just laws and regulations, paying taxes to support the government, and when necessary defending our nation from attack.

Patriotism is the virtue of love of one's country. This virtue is in keeping with Christianity because it is natural and good for us to love our country. But patriotism is more than flag-waving. It is dedication to the promotion of the true welfare of the whole country and its citizens.

As citizens, we should be concerned about the health and well-being of our society. We should work to establish just conditions that allow all people to have what they have a right to have. If there is an unjust practice or an immoral law, then we must do all we can to overturn it. We must work within the structure of our government to establish justice for all and to make that justice secure.

Just because the state declares an action to be legal does not mean the action is morally good. Sometimes things that the state declares "legal" really violate natural law and the rights of others. It was once "legal" to enslave people

of a certain race, but that did not make it right or just. It is wrong to buy and sell people as if they were property. All human beings have the same basic dignity as persons. This means that they have rights, which the state is supposed to protect, and which it may not take away.

We have today the grave evil of "legalized" abortion. The state has declared a seriously immoral and unjust act to be acceptable and "within the law." It has declared it "legal" to take the life of an unborn child, even though the innocent child has the same basic God-given right to life as every other human being. We may not support such a declaration of the state because it is contrary to God's law and the state's duty to protect the rights of all people. We should do all in our power to change such a law or other laws that violate people's basic rights. "We must obey God rather than men" (Acts 5:29).

Across Boundaries

As followers of Christ we must not think only of our own nation. We must be concerned about the needs of all people. Many people and nations are oppressed and deprived of basic human rights by severe poverty or by lack of freedom. Just as there are different forms of good governments, so there are governments that are bad and threaten the well-being of their citizens. Wealthier and stronger countries have a responsibility to help these oppressed nations. As citizens we must encourage our government to do what is possible to help people in need.

Above all we must remember to pray for our country and its leaders.

Q. 37 *Why must we obey those in authority?*

We must obey those in authority because this authority comes from God. To oppose it is to oppose the authority of God (CCC 2197, 2234).

Q. 38 *What must we do if men in authority command us to violate God's law?*

If men in authority command us to violate God's law, we must obey God rather than men (CCC 2242).

Q. 39 *What is the duty of a citizen?*

The duty of a citizen is to contribute to the good of society by obeying all just laws, paying taxes, voting, and defending one's own country (CCC 2239–40).

Saint Thomas More

In the year 1535 Sir Thomas More was beheaded by order of the king of England and his court of law. Thomas More had been a friend to King Henry the Eighth and had even held the office of Lord Chancellor, second in power to the king. What had Sir Thomas More done that caused his one-time friend and ruler to have him put to death? He had chosen to obey God's law rather than man's. King Henry the Eighth had declared himself to be the supreme head of the Church in England. Thomas More knew that such a declaration was a violation of the law of God, and so he would not accept it, even if his refusal meant death.

Saint Thomas More had been a great statesman and had dedicated himself to the service of his king and country. But he knew that God's law was above the King's, and so he was willing to die "the King's good servant, but God's first." For suffering this martyrdom, Thomas More has been declared a saint by the Church.

CHAPTER 10

Church Authority–
Our Fathers in Faith

"He who hears you hears me, and he who rejects you rejects me, and he who rejects me rejects him who sent me."

Luke 10:16

Besides our parents and the state there is another authority over us that demands our obedience. That is the Catholic Church as founded on earth by Jesus.

Jesus gave to the Church its mission to save souls and to teach all men the truths of the Faith. He chose his Apostles to govern the Church as a body. Establishing the Church was the means Jesus chose to remain with us always and to lead us to his heavenly Kingdom, our final goal.

The Vicar of Christ

Jesus is the head or ruler of his Church, which is his Body. He is the one who has given the authority to the Pope to rule the Church on his behalf. It was to Saint Peter, the first Pope, that Jesus said: "I will give you the keys of the kingdom of heaven, and whatever you bind on earth shall be bound in heaven, and whatever you loose on earth shall be loosed in heaven" (Mt 16:19).

Including our present Pope, there have been more than 260 Popes. The authority of Saint Peter has been passed on to each one down to our own day.

The mission of the Church is to preach the gospel and lead all people to holiness. The Pope is chiefly responsible for seeing that this mission is accomplished. It is for this purpose that the Pope and bishops, as successors of the Apostles, have the authority to make the **precepts** or rules and disciplines of the Church.

A bishop is the chief authority in his own diocese. (A diocese is the part of the Church led by a bishop.) The bishop has this authority as long as he remains in union with the Pope. The bishop shares some of his authority with the priests and deacons of his diocese. In this way, Christ governs his people, the Church, through the Pope, the other bishops, and the priests and deacons under the bishops. These ordained ministers share in Jesus' authority in order to help the whole Church, the Body of Christ, to be holy and to spread the message of Jesus to others.

The Church is carefully governed so that it may be clearly recognized by the unity of its faith and worship.

Unity of Faith

To make sure that the Faith is taught correctly and the gospel preached to all without error, the Pope has the authority to declare what is to be taught. He answers moral questions and addresses himself to any current problem which affects the lives of Christians. The Pope does this in his speeches, encyclicals, letters, and declarations. The bishops do the same in their dioceses, usually through pastoral letters that are made available to everyone in the world by the Church.

One in the Sacraments

Since it is through the Sacraments that the Church fulfills her role in sanctifying men, it is necessary that they be administered in a consistent way in all times and places. The Church determines what is required to receive each Sacrament: for example, how old a person must be and what the accompanying ceremony should include. The Church also sets the requirements for becoming and remaining a member of the Church. The Pope and the other bishops make judgments about moral

---

Precepts of the Church

1. "You shall attend Mass on Sundays and on Holy Days of Obligation and rest from servile labor." The first precept requires us to keep holy the day of the Lord's Resurrection; to worship God by participating in Mass every Sunday and Holy Day of Obligation; to avoid those activities that would hinder renewal of soul and body on the Lord's day.

2. "You shall confess your sins at least once a year." The second precept requires us to lead a sacramental life; to receive the Sacrament of Penance regularly—minimally, to receive the Sacrament of Penance at least once a year (annual confession is obligatory only if serious sin is involved) in preparation to receive Holy Communion.

3. "You shall receive the Sacrament of the Eucharist at least during the Easter season." The third precept requires us to receive Holy Communion frequently; minimally, to receive Holy Communion once during the Easter season.

4. "You shall observe the days of fasting and abstinence established by the Church." The fourth precept requires us to do penance, including abstaining from meat and fasting from food on the appointed days.

5. "You shall help to provide for the needs of the Church." The fifth precept requires us to strengthen and support the Church—one's own parish community and parish priests, the worldwide Church, and the Pope.

(CCC 2042–43)

and social issues when these things affect people's basic rights or their salvation.

Holy Mother Church

The Church is often referred to as our Holy Mother Church. This shows the attitude we should have toward the Church and her leaders. Like all mothers, the Church exists to give us life and to provide for our well-being and development until we reach our final goal. We should have great reverence and love for the Church because Jesus gave us the Church as a sign of his love for us.

Words to Know:

Vicar of Christ   precepts

Q. 40   *Why does the Church have the authority to make laws and precepts?*

The Church has the authority to make laws and precepts because she has received this authority from Jesus Christ through his Apostles. Thus he who disobeys the Church disobeys God himself (CCC 2035–37).

Q. 41   *Who can make laws and precepts in the Church?*

The bishops in union with the Pope, as successors of the Apostles, can make laws and precepts in the Church. Jesus Christ said to them: "He who hears you hears me, and he who rejects you rejects me, and he who rejects me rejects him who sent me" (CCC 2041, Lk 10:16).

Q. 42   *Must members of the Church obey the precepts of the Church?*

Yes, members of the Church must obey the precepts of the Church (CCC 2037).

CHAPTER 11

Respect Life

"You shall not kill."

Exodus 20:13

Man is a creature composed of body and soul. Some people go about their business as if they had never heard of the soul. The truth is that both body and soul are essential to the human being. Though separated by death, the body and the soul are destined to be reunited at the resurrection on the Last Day.

Because we have souls made in the image of God we can share in God's life. We call this supernatural life because it is above our natural life here on earth. We can possess it only as God's gift.

The Fifth Commandment, "You shall not kill," gives us the responsibility to care for both the natural and supernatural life that God has given to us and all men.

Right to Life

Since God is the giver of life, no man or group of men has the right to take innocent human life. To do so is **murder**. And murder is a serious crime and a very serious sin, a mortal sin. Murder violates the God-given right to life of the one who is murdered. Many people today think they can take the matter of life and death into their own hands. For example, many people ignore or accept the murder of millions of unborn babies in our own nation and around the world. An estimated fifty million unborn babies are killed every year by abortion.

Another area where there is a weakening of respect for human life is euthanasia, or "mercy killing." It is never justified. A sick or elderly person must be given the normal or ordinary treatment to keep him alive. To do otherwise would be murder. Extraordinary treatment is another matter—it is not required.

These days there is more and more pressure for euthanasia. Men are taking the beginning and the end of life into their own hands.

The Fifth Commandment makes it clear that it is wrong to take innocent life. Some people maintain that all killing is wrong and never allowable, no matter what the reasons. But there are certain situations in which killing is not the same thing as murder. The most obvious examples of this are the taking of life in self-defense, capital punishment, and just wars. The Church has never condemned these acts as murder. But since every act of taking human life is a serious matter, we must always look to the Church for guidance in these areas.

Murder is not the only violation of the Fifth Commandment. It would be a mortal sin to injure someone seriously by careless driving. It is wrong *not to care* whether our actions may injure others.

Suicide, the act of killing oneself, is always seriously wrong. God alone is the master of our lives, and we are too precious in his sight to toss our lives away. If someone commits suicide without full knowledge and consent, his responsibility before God is lessened. But even if a man is not blameworthy, his action is still wrong.

It is also wrong not to take proper care of ourselves, with proper diet, exercise, and rest. We should avoid risking our lives by doing foolish stunts when we are encouraged by a dare or a desire to show off. We should protect ourselves from disease by sensible habits of cleanliness and dress. We should avoid impatience and carelessness that may lead to accident or injury.

The sin of eating and drinking too much is a sin that can harm the body; so can the improper use of medicines and other drugs. Taking a little less food and drink than we want is a small but sensible restraint on our bodies and an excellent form of self-denial. As we have seen, some self-denial is a necessary part of Christian living. We have considered acts against the Fifth Commandment that harm people's physical well-being, such as murder, suicide, and not taking care of your health. In the next chapter, we will consider acts that cause other kinds of harm.

Words to Know:

murder   suicide

"Any one who hates his brother is a murderer, and you know that no murderer has eternal life abiding in him."

1 John 3:15

Q. 43   ***What does the Fifth Commandment require?***
The Fifth Commandment requires that we respect all human life from the moment of conception to natural death, as well as the spiritual life of grace in human beings (CCC 2258, 2287).

Q. 44   ***What does the Fifth Commandment forbid?***
The Fifth Commandment forbids *direct and intentional killing*. This includes murder, the taking of innocent life, curses, and scandal (CCC 2268, 2284).

CHAPTER 12

Charity toward All

"If you love those who love you, what credit is that to you? For even sinners love those who love them. . . . But love your enemies, and do good, and lend, expecting nothing in return; and your reward will be great, and you will be sons of the Most High; for he is kind to the ungrateful and the selfish."

Luke 6:32, 35

The law of love—"Love your neighbor as yourself"—is closely connected to the Fifth Commandment. We have seen many striking and violent offenses against this commandment. There are other more common offenses in which persons are not hurt physically but harm is done. Such actions are far from Christian.

Goodwill

Christ preached goodwill toward all, friends and enemies alike. This is what he meant when he said, "Love your enemies." It is hard enough not to strike back when we are hurt; it is even harder to respond with love.

But how do we know if we love our enemies? Do we have to love them with our feelings? Do I have to *feel* this love for my enemy? Not necessarily. We will not be held accountable for the absence of such feeling, but we are responsible for *goodwill*.

I will know whether I love my enemy if I want what is good for him regardless of how I may feel. We must willingly want what is good for others; the will is the center of love. I may not *like* my enemy, but if I wish him

well and treat him well, I am fulfilling Christ's words, "Love your enemies" (Mt 5:44).

One thing that can get in the way of goodwill is anger. When we lose our tempers, we say things and do things to get back at others, to *hurt* them. How terrible, then, the gift of speech can be! We can make it a weapon by yelling at someone, calling someone names, or **cursing**. All these things come under the Fifth Commandment, which prohibits deliberate injury to another human being in any way.

Closely linked to anger is hatred. To hate someone is to wish evil to someone, or even to wish that he did not exist! It may be conceived in the heat of anger but persist even when the feelings have cooled down because, like love, it is willed, although it is the very opposite of love. This is ill will, a wish that another person be hurt and suffer, perhaps even be killed.

Saint John wrote: "Any one who hates his brother is a murderer" (1 Jn 3:15). Indeed, we can have our neighbor dead and buried in our minds without ever doing anything to him, but because of our hatred we are like murderers!

All this can start, perhaps, because we lost our tempers and began to nurture ill will. The danger of anger is that we do things blindly, unaware of the evil in our thoughts, careless of the bitter enmity we may provoke with our stinging words, perhaps stirred even to the point of physical violence.

Jesus left no doubt about the sinfulness of anger when he said in the Sermon on the Mount:

> You have heard that it was said to the men of old, "You shall not kill; and whoever kills shall be liable to judgment." But I say to you that every one who is angry with his brother shall be liable to judgment; whoever insults his brother shall be liable to the council. . . (Mt 5:21–22).

When someone has hurt us in some way, we are required to refrain not only from striking back but also from harboring ill will toward him. We must do something positive. Jesus says: "Love your enemies, do good to those who hate you, bless those who curse you, pray for those who abuse you" (Lk 6:27–28).

And Saint Paul wrote: "Bless those who persecute you; bless and do not curse them. . . . Repay no one evil for evil, but take thought for what is noble in the sight of all" (Rom 12:14, 17).

Here is a thought which can take a lot of the sting out of harsh words and ill treatment: try offering the pain to God for the salvation of the one who hurts you. No matter how you feel, surely you would like to see your enemy in heaven someday.

In addition, if you get the opportunity, show respect and consideration to your enemy. Suddenly you may see things through the eyes of Jesus. How many times he was insulted! No doubt he felt the pain, like every other man—perhaps even more—but he knew that the men who insulted him were wonderful creations and that no matter how bad they were, they were continually being called to a new life of grace.

Not all anger is wrong. There is such a thing as *just anger*; for instance, when Jesus chased the money-changers from the temple or when he rebuked hypocrites. Righteous anger can help us to stand up for the rights of oppressed persons or come to the defense of those suffering unjust aggression. It may help us to speak up for someone who isn't getting his rights —ourselves or others. Finally, a holy anger may motivate us to fight for a very important cause —like working in the pro-life movement to end the evil of abortion or against other injustices.

Scandal

There is a special case of bad will which Jesus condemned with utmost severity: **scandal**. It is a fully conscious and deliberate bad example or encouragement that could lead another person into sin. This sin endangers someone else's eternal destiny. There can be no greater lack of charity to our neighbor.

Any sinful act could lead another into sin, but anything said or done with the knowledge that it may weaken the faith or destroy the spiritual life of another is scandal. The person who gives scandal is responsible for all the sins into which others are led. Jesus said:

> Whoever receives one such child in my name receives me; but whoever causes one of these little ones who believe in me to sin, it would be better for him to have a great millstone fastened round his neck and to be drowned in the depth of the sea (Mt 18:5–6).

Forgive Us, as We Forgive Others

On the Cross Jesus prayed to his Father, "Father, forgive them; for they know not what they do" (Lk 23:34). As followers of Christ we must be willing to forgive those who hurt us. And we must also govern our thoughts and actions so that we do not injure other people physically or spiritually.

Words to Know:
cursing   scandal

"Let all bitterness and wrath and anger and clamor and slander be put away from you, with all malice, and be kind to one another, tenderhearted, forgiving one another, as God in Christ forgave you."

Ephesians 4:31–32

Q. 45   *What is scandal?*

Scandal is the sin of leading others into sin by the example of our action (CCC 2284).

Q. 46   *Does the Fifth Commandment require us to have goodwill toward all, even our enemies?*

Yes, the Fifth Commandment requires us to have goodwill toward all, even our enemies (CCC 2262).

CHAPTER 13

The Sacred Flame

"You shall not commit adultery. . . . You shall not covet your neighbor's house; you shall not covet your neighbor's wife, or his manservant, or his maidservant, or his ox, or his donkey, or anything that is your neighbor's."

Exodus 20:14, 17

All men were made by God in his image and likeness. And all of us are known and loved by God as distinct individuals. It is this special relation each of us has to God that is the foundation of our dignity as persons and the source of our rights as human beings.

Everyone has this dignity as a child of God, and so every individual is worthy of our respect, for each person is made by God to be loved by him and to have God's life within. We ourselves have this dignity, of course, and so we must also have respect for ourselves—self-respect.

To maintain our self-respect and respect for others we have to do what we know is right and avoid what we know is wrong. To do this we need to develop our self-control and overcome our weaknesses.

The Sixth and Ninth Commandments, "You shall not commit adultery" and "You shall not covet your neighbor's wife," demand from us that respect which we are to have for ourselves and for others, and in a special way for those things that belong to married life and the family.

Be Fruitful

When a seed is planted in the earth there are certain laws that govern its development, and if the conditions are right it grows into a specific plant, whether it is a sunflower or an olive tree. Then it will produce seeds after its own kind which will propagate the species—that is, reproduce or multiply. God finds this very good; it is the way he designed things.

Animals propagate as well. Like the flowers, when conditions are right everything happens according to certain laws and there is no misuse of these powers. We don't have to preach self-control to plants and animals because they act through instinct.

But man is different. Like plants and animals, he reproduces and multiplies and fills the earth. This is what God wants, for Scripture says:

So God created man in his own image, in the image of God he created him; male and female he created them. And God blessed them, and God said to them, "Be fruitful and multiply, and fill the earth. . ." (Gen 1:27–28).

But, unlike the rest of visible creation, man does not multiply blindly, following the seasons, like plants, or by instinct, like animals. These creatures are not free to make decisions about their reproductive powers. Man *is* free. This is an aspect of man's dignity. It is also a possible source of abuse.

Man may have very powerful urges, but he is not led blindly by his instincts. Man is called to cooperate with God in a plan that is not recorded in his genes or in his blood but is revealed by God in his commandments—specifically, the Sixth and Ninth Commandments.

Many people look upon these two commandments as restrictions, but we can think about them in the following way. The seed that becomes a sunflower is guided to this fulfillment by a biochemical blueprint invented by God. Though we do not see it, God, who holds the sacred flame of *all* life, has a blueprint for our fulfillment too. Man should thus follow God's plan in the use of his reproductive powers. If God can lead the sunflower to full beauty from a seed, then he can lead a man

to fullness of life by the laws he has given us, though we may see only a little of his plan.

When you are about to plant a seed and water it, you do not have to remind it to trust God; the seed knows all that, so to speak. It is *man* who needs to be reminded to trust God!

Laws of Life

All this is said to point out the proper beauty and nature of the human reproductive powers. The Sixth Commandment guides us in our actions, the Ninth in our thoughts and desires. It is important to remember that all our actions start in our mind, and so we should see the importance of properly directing our thoughts and desires.

Put simply, God reserved the pleasures and joys of human sexuality for marriage. Any use of these powers outside of marriage is a serious sin. God plans to give those who marry an actual share in the creation of a new human being; God creates the soul and the human parents help fashion the body. Does it seem unreasonable, then, for God to require that men use these powers in the right way? God created us male or female. Being male or female is important to who we are as human beings. It is important to use our sexuality according to the will of God, who created and loves us.

The love between a man and a woman, made fruitful and blessed by God in marriage, lovingly brings a new child into a family, where he will have the attention and devotion of both father and mother. It is to assure such conditions for children that God has designed human sexuality to be enjoyed only in marriage, and then only in the proper way. Society is filled to overflowing with the problems, evils, and afflictions caused by disregard for God's wise guidance and authority.

The proper use or control of our sexual powers is called **chastity**, which is a virtue or good habit. Chastity requires that we practice self-denial and self-control. A person who has the virtue of chastity is chaste. A chaste person will avoid anything that might be a temptation to sin against purity, such as indecent books, magazines, video games, and movies. Our purity is something to be protected. To safeguard it we are forbidden to commit any act in thought or deed that is impure and shameful. **Impurity** is sexual thought or action that is against the Sixth or Ninth Commandments.

What God requires of us is purity of heart and soul, all in keeping with our dignity as his children.

Saint Maria Goretti

In 1950, at Rome, a girl who had died at the age of twelve was declared a saint. She had been stabbed to death because she refused to commit an act of impurity. Her name is Maria Goretti.

Maria was born in Ancona, Italy, in 1890. Her father was a tenant farmer; his family moved around a lot as he looked for work. He died when Maria was ten.

Maria never had the chance to go to school; she never learned to read or write. But she was carefully instructed in the Catholic Faith by her mother, Assunta. She received her first Holy Communion when she was twelve.

Assunta had advised her daughter Maria as she had all her children: "Never, at any cost, never must you sin!" Maria never forgot.

Shortly after her first Communion, a nine-teen-year-old boy who worked with Maria's family wanted her to be unchaste and threatened her with a knife. When she would not give in, he stabbed her to death.

Many years later, the man who had killed her repented and turned to a life devoted to God. He joined those who sought her canonization.

Maria is the great saint of purity for our difficult age.

Words to Know:
chastity   impurity

Purity prepares the soul for love, and love confirms the soul in purity.

—Blessed Cardinal Newman

Q. 47   *What does the Sixth Commandment require?*
The Sixth Commandment requires us to be chaste in our actions and words (CCC 2331, 2336).

Q. 48   *What does the Sixth Commandment forbid?*
The Sixth Commandment forbids unchastity, or impurity, of any kind, including looking at immoral pictures, movies, games, and shows (CCC 2351, 2354, 2396, 2523).

Q. 49   *What does the Ninth Commandment require?*
The Ninth Commandment requires us to be chaste in our thoughts and desires (CCC 2517, 2532–33).

Q. 50   *What does the Ninth Commandment forbid?*
The Ninth Commandment forbids unchaste or impure thoughts and desires (CCC 2520, 2528–30).

Ownership

"You shall not steal."

Exodus 20:15

God gave to the human race the earth and its resources, to use, to enjoy, to appreciate, and to share freely with one another. People use these goods of creation to keep themselves from poverty and to meet other basic human needs.

You will find very few things around you that someone does not own. The things around us may be owned by a group of people like a company, or by a larger community such as a city, state, or nation, or by a single person. Every person has the right to own property; groups have the same right. This requires respect for the right of ownership; all have the right to have their possessions safe from theft, damage, and destruction.

These rights are protected by the Seventh Commandment: "You shall not **steal**".

This commandment tells us how to treat other peoples' belongings. God commands us not to take what belongs to another. If I take your shoes without asking you, I am guilty of theft. To be free from guilt I must return what I have stolen or replace it if I can, as well as confess my sin if the matter is serious. If I purposely damage or destroy property, justice demands that I make restitution—that is, pay for the damage.

We must have nothing to do with stolen property, even if we didn't steal it ourselves.

Neither can we claim to own something that belongs to someone else—for example, when one student copies another's homework. Such a student is guilty of both stealing and lying, since he presents the work as his own.

On Loan

We have duties and obligations when we make rightful use of another's property by permission. Perhaps we have borrowed a CD to see how we like it before buying one of our own. Then we must return it in the same condition in which we received it. If we have damaged it, we must replace it. So too, in a store, we must handle merchandise with care and be honest if we damage something. We must always pay back in full all loans and debts; if we don't we are stealing.

The Seventh Commandment also forbids any kind of deception or breach of contract in our dealings with others' property. This is called **fraud**. There is another evil practice called **usury** in which someone lends money at an excessively high rate of interest. This is a very bad thing. Someone who practices usury is making money out of another person's great need.

We are also required to be just in payment for services or goods bought. We must always pay a worker what he has earned.

The Seventh Commandment also requires respect for creation. This includes mineral resources, plants, and animals. We should respect and appreciate such gifts and use them according to God's laws. We should also take care to make sure future generations can appreciate and use these gifts.

The Tenth Commandment, "You shall not covet your neighbor's goods," is meant to direct our desire for possessions.

There are two very common ways in which people break this commandment: **envy** and **avarice**. Both reveal that something is wrong with the way a person looks upon material goods. Envy is being resentful of another's success. The envious man is unhappy because he wants what another man has. Avarice is like greed. The avaricious man has an excessive desire for wealth. He always wants more, no matter how much he already has.

Justice and Charity

There are certain societies in which the right to own private property is denied. However, the right to private property is acknowledged by God in the Ten Commandments. He would not condemn stealing if no one were to own anything.

> Be not anxious about what you have, but about what you are.
>
> —Pope Saint Gregory

Stealing is wrong because it is unjust. Thus, justice is the virtue that protects personal possessions. Justice obliges me to make restitution if I steal. It obliges my employer to pay me my due wage and obliges me to earn it with honest labor.

But the right to private property, protected by justice, is not enough for the happy life of a society; charity is needed.

For instance, the right to property may be acknowledged by everyone, while at the same time some persons have more than they need —even much more—and others do not have even a minimum required by human dignity.

If I have many possessions should they be taken away and given to the poor? No, but should I forget the poor? Charity requires me to share what I have with those who need decent food, clothing, and shelter. Such almsgiving is a work of justice as well as charity, and it is pleasing to God. One reason God allows us to have possessions is in order for us to share them with others.

Every human being is made in God's image and deserves respect as a person. This is where justice comes in. Justice involves giving everyone his due, what he has a right to receive. Every human being has a right to food, clothing, and shelter. Of course the ordinary way we should obtain these things is through our work. But if circumstances do not make it possible for someone to obtain these things through his labor, then other people are obliged to help him from their excess.

If people are in extreme need and they have no choice, then the taking of what is necessary to maintain life is not stealing. In that case, it is unreasonable and unjust for someone to refuse to provide such people with what they need to live.

Jesus identifies himself with the poor when he says:

> "Come, O blessed of my Father, inherit the kingdom prepared for you from the foundation of the world; for I was hungry and you gave me food, I was thirsty and you gave me drink, I was a stranger and you welcomed me, I was naked and you clothed me, I was sick and you visited me, I was in prison and you came to me." Then the righteous will answer him, "Lord, when did we see you hungry and feed you, or thirsty and give you drink? And when did we see you a stranger and welcome you, or naked and clothe you? And when did we see you sick or in prison and visit you?" And the King will answer them, "Truly, I say to you, as you did it to one of the least of these my brethren, you did it to me" (Mt 25:34–40).

In this way, Jesus shows how God blesses those who help the poor. When we help the poor, we show our love for them and for Jesus himself. We should do what we can to see to it that everyone has what he needs to live a decent human life.

Spirit of Poverty

Saint Francis of Assisi was known as "the poor man." He won this title by owning little more than the shirt on his back. If he was asked about his circumstances he would often reply that he was married to Lady Poverty. Francis meant that he loved poverty and never wanted to own anything.

This was a great shock to his father, who was a rich cloth merchant and had great plans for his son. But God had other plans. Francis' father, Pietro Bernardone, did not accept God's plans gracefully. The result was that father and son parted company. Pietro's plans were ruined, but a whole new world opened up for Francis. He roamed the hillsides of Assisi; he walked the byways praising God; he lived in the open; he prayed long hours; he begged; and he rebuilt a mountain chapel that had fallen into disrepair. Soon others began following him, until finally a great religious order grew up around Francis' example.

Saint Francis is set before us as one who had the right attitude toward material possessions. We should not set our hearts on riches. Few of us are called to be as poor as Francis, but our Lord addressed the following words to all men:

"No one can serve two masters; for either he will hate the one and love the other, or he will be devoted to the one and despise the other. You cannot serve God and mammon" (Mt 6:24).

Jesus means that a person who has his heart set on material possessions will not be able to pay attention to the Kingdom of God. Instead of looking for chances to serve God, to pray, or to study our Lord's words and example, such a person will be looking for chances to collect more riches. (This may mean piling up much more than one needs.) One cannot have one's mind on both things—God and money. It must be one or the other.

Serving God wholeheartedly, of course, need not mean choosing Lady Poverty, like Francis; but it cannot mean choosing riches instead of God's plan, like his father. We should try to be content with what we have and take reasonable care of our interests.

Words to Know:
steal   fraud   usury   envy   avarice

"Keep your life free from love of money, and be content with what you have."   *Hebrews 13:5*

Q. 51   *What does the Seventh Commandment require us to do?*
The Seventh Commandment requires us to respect the property of others, to return anything we have stolen or borrowed, to repair damages for which we are responsible, to pay our debts, and to pay a just wage to those who work for us (CCC 2411–12).

Q. 52   *What does the Seventh Commandment forbid?*
The Seventh Commandment forbids unjustly taking or keeping our neighbor's property. Sins against the Seventh Commandment include theft, damage of property, usury, and fraud (CCC 2408–9).

Q. 53   *What does the Tenth Commandment require us to do?*
The Tenth Commandment requires us to be just and moderate in the desire to improve our own condition of life. We are called to suffer with patience the hardships and other difficulties permitted by the Lord for our good (CCC 2545).

Q. 54   *What does the Tenth Commandment forbid?*
The Tenth Commandment forbids wrongly desiring what others have and excessively desiring riches and power (CCC 2536, 2538).

CHAPTER 15

Backed by Truth

"You shall not bear false witness against your neighbor."

Exodus 20:16

The Eighth Commandment requires that we speak the truth always, but especially in matters involving the good name and honor of others. Truth is very important to us. If men were not truthful it would be impossible for us to live together.

When he was on trial before Pilate, Jesus said: "For this I was born, and for this I have come into the world, to bear witness to the truth. Every one who is of the truth hears my voice" (Jn 18:37). Pilate said to him, "What is truth?" (Jn 18:38). Evidently Pilate, who may at one time have been concerned about truth, about the meaning of life, about right and wrong, no longer cared, or had given up on it and decided there was no such thing.

But our Lord had come as a witness to the truth. And Pilate could not help being impressed. This is perhaps what led him to make a few weak attempts to save our Lord's life; but, as we know, Pilate gave in under pressure and agreed to a lie by condemning Jesus.

We all know what harm can be done just by one lie. The Eighth Commandment tells us we must never tell even a single lie. But it also directs all our powers of communication. We are obliged to speak the truth and must never intend to deceive another when he has the right to the truth. We must not bear **false witness**.

Lying

A lie is a deliberate attempt to mislead others. It is always sinful. We may not lie to get out of trouble, to cover up for a friend, or to get into a movie. Even if what we want is good, we may not lie to get it.

We can be strongly tempted to lie sometimes—it can seem so simple and so harmless. But we must always tell the truth to those who have a right to know.

Hypocrisy

One kind of untruthfulness is hypocrisy, which is when someone pretends to be better than he really is or pretends to believe something he really denies just to impress people. Jesus condemned this sin many times. However, it is not wrong to be on one's best behavior with those on whom one wishes to make a good impression.

Promises and Oaths

An important aspect of honesty is keeping one's word. One makes one's word true by living up to it. Keeping one's word means telling the truth about one's future actions.

In taking an oath in a courtroom one promises to tell the truth with God as one's witness. This is very serious. It is always a serious sin to lie in an important matter, but to lie under oath before God is much worse. Such a lie is called perjury.

Another's Good Name

There are times when we may be telling the truth and still sin. We must always speak the truth if we speak at all, but sometimes it is more prudent or charitable for us to remain silent. There are even times when we must not tell what we know to be true, for to do so would be wrong.

We have a precious possession that we may take for granted: our good name or reputation. We may hardly think of it, unless it is endangered. But if it is hurt or lost we see how precious it is to us. "A good name is to be chosen rather than great riches" (Prov 22:1). Regaining a good name once it is lost is very difficult; just think how hard it must be for an ex-convict to find a job. To damage a person's reputation is a serious matter. Therefore, one must have a very good reason for revealing anything about a person which would hurt his good name.

As for ourselves, we should take care to be worthy of a good reputation—not by seeking fame and renown, but by loving God and our neighbor and by being known as faithful followers of Christ.

There may be times when we are called upon to reveal what we know about someone—for instance, in legal proceedings—but we must be very careful about what we do with damaging facts, even if they are true.

How much worse, then, is a damaging story which is not true! Irresponsible or malicious use of the truth to harm another is called

detraction and is a serious sin. The use of lies to hurt someone is called calumny or **slander** and is an even greater sin. There is a grave obligation to repair the damage done by any of these sins.

Rash Judgment

Besides being careful in what we say about someone, we must also be careful in what we think. There is a sin called **rash judgment**, which is to judge another person's character without enough evidence. This does not mean that we may never make a judgment, but that we must be very careful about it. Otherwise someone may lose our esteem without a good reason. We should be very slow to judge another.

Gossip

As a rule, we should not talk about the faults of others unless there is a good and important reason to do so. **Gossip** usually consists of talking about the faults of others or exaggerating them. People who gossip may deal with facts, but they destroy another person's good name to satisfy idle curiosity. We must not be willing even to listen to people who gossip about others.

Secrets

We must keep any promise we have made, including the promise to keep a secret. If someone tells us a secret, or if we find out something that must be kept secret for another person's good, then we must be silent about what we have learned.

Our power of speech is a precious gift, a gift that must not be used to hurt others! Jesus says:

> I tell you, on the day of judgment men will render account for every careless word they utter; for by your words you will be justified, and by your words you will be condemned (Mt 12:36–37).

Words to Know:
false witness   detraction   slander
rash judgment   gossip

"Let no evil talk come out of your mouths, but only such as is good for edifying, as fits the occasion, that it may impart grace to those who hear."

Ephesians 4:29

Q. 55   *What does the Eighth Commandment require?*

The Eighth Commandment requires us to speak the truth responsibly and to avoid rash judgment of our neighbors' actions (CCC 2464, 2475).

Q. 56   *What does the Eighth Commandment forbid?*

The Eighth Commandment forbids all deliberate falsehood and unjust damage to another person's reputation. Sins against the Eighth Commandment include bearing false witness, slander, lying, detraction, flattery, unfounded suspicion, and rash judgment (CCC 2464, 2476–77).

Q. 57   *What must one do who has damaged his neighbor's good reputation by accusing him falsely or speaking badly of him?*

One who has damaged his neighbor's good reputation by false accusation or speaking badly of him must repair the damage he has done, so far as he is able (CCC 2487).

Q. 58   *What is the supreme witness of the truth?*

Martyrdom is the supreme witness given to the truth of faith, bearing witness unto death (CCC 2473).

CHAPTER 16

The Beatitudes

"O Lᴏʀᴅ of hosts, blessed is the man who trusts in you!"

Psalm 84:12

When he was about thirty years old, Jesus began his public life with his baptism by Saint John the Baptist in the Jordan River. When he was baptized, the Holy Spirit descended like a dove and rested upon Jesus. A voice from the heavens said: "This is my beloved Son, with whom I am well pleased" (Mt 3:17).

Following his baptism, Jesus was led by the Spirit into the wilderness, where he prayed and fasted for forty days and overcame the devil's temptations.

After this, Jesus set out to preach the Good News of God's Kingdom. He was a teacher, a reformer, and a miracle worker, and he was the perfect living example of everything he taught. He even raised the dead to life. He taught everywhere: in the fields, on the roads, on the hillsides, in the synagogues, by lakes, and even from a boat. He often taught in parables, using for examples things people used and saw every day, from the lilies of the field to the sparrows of the air.

Jesus didn't come to abolish the Old Law but to fulfill it in the New. He built on the Ten Commandments and the "you shall not" prohibitions by giving positive exhortations to live the Christian life. Among these exhortations are those called the Beatitudes. They sum up the blessings and joys in store for people who follow Jesus and his way of life. A **beatitude** is a blessing or special happiness of a spiritual nature.

Jesus emphasized that these blessings are open to everyone, no matter how poor or uneducated or sick or seemingly unwanted a person may be. This contradicted the Scribes and Pharisees, who taught that poverty or bad health was a punishment and a sign of God's disfavor.

The Beatitudes

"Blessed are the poor in spirit, for theirs is the kingdom of heaven" (Mt 5:3).

The poor in spirit are those who may have material possessions but who are ready to give them up when self-sacrifice is called for. They value heavenly treasure above everything else and never lose sight of it.

You may remember the rich young man who turned away from following Jesus because this man was attached to his many possessions. The poor in spirit do just the opposite: when Jesus calls, they leave all things to follow him. Because their hearts are not filled with things of earth, God fills their hearts with himself.

"Blessed are those who mourn, for they shall be comforted" (Mt 5:4).

Mourning, in this beatitude, means sorrow for sin and sorrow over the loss, by separation or by death, of someone dear to us.

Jesus promises the sorrowful that they will get the strength they need to stand firm in their trials and troubles and even to grow through their sorrows in their friendship with God.

"Blessed are the meek, for they shall inherit the earth" (Mt 5:5).

The meek are those who are truly humble and kind. They don't think of themselves as being better than other people. They accept and recognize the gifts God has given them with gratitude and patience and without complaint.

"Blessed are those who hunger and thirst for righteousness, for they shall be satisfied" (Mt 5:6).

Blessed is the heart that wants what God wants! If we desire to be righteous and holy, Jesus will help us and our desire will be fulfilled. Jesus promises joy to those who do God's will.

"Blessed are the merciful, for they shall obtain mercy" (Mt 5:7).

Mercy is love shown to those in need as well as those who have been unjust and ungrateful. The merciful provide for the needs of others, forgive others their offenses, and show kindness and compassion toward the sinner. They, in turn, will receive mercy from God. Jesus said: "If you forgive men their trespasses, your heavenly Father also will forgive you" (Mt 6:14).

"Blessed are the pure in heart, for they shall see God" (Mt 5:8).

The pure in heart are those who live chaste lives and are free of all excessive love of earthly things. They have put God first in their lives. Because they are single-hearted, they can feel God's presence in this life and will see him face to face in the next.

"Blessed are the peacemakers, for they shall be called sons of God" (Mt 5:9).

Psalm 133 begins: "Behold, how good and how pleasant it is when brothers dwell together in unity!"

Peacemakers go out of their way to remove the obstacles that keep men apart. They work especially hard to bring sinners back to God.

Jesus promises that peacemakers will be God's special children here on earth and will enjoy heavenly glory in the family of the saints.

"Blessed are those who are persecuted for righteousness' sake, for theirs is the kingdom of heaven" (Mt 5:10).

"Blessed are you when men revile you and persecute you and utter all kinds of evil against you falsely on my account" (Mt 5:11).

Jesus suffered everything to witness to the truth. If we are persecuted because we are loyal to Jesus and his Church, we will know a little of what he suffered on the Cross to free us from sin and death. But we will also share in the joy of his Resurrection, his gift of eternal life with God.

* * *

The Beatitudes are the counsels of the New Testament; instead of being prohibitions, they are positive exhortations to live in a way that keeps us close to Jesus Christ. Each beatitude has attached to it a promise of great rewards.

Perhaps you have been thinking how difficult this is—how impossible, even, for human strength alone to live up to. You're right—it *is* hard!

That is why Christ has left us a great source of divine power in the Holy Eucharist. If we take the Ten Commandments and the Beatitudes seriously and desire to live up to them, we will feel the call to unite ourselves to Christ by receiving the Holy Eucharist often—perhaps even daily. And we will be well on our way to living the authentic Christian life.

Word to Know:

beatitude

Q. 59 *How are the Beatitudes related to the Ten Commandments?*
The Beatitudes are the fulfillment of the Ten Commandments and reveal the goal of human existence. The Beatitudes promise the reign of the Kingdom of God, which is at the heart of Jesus' teaching (CCC 1716, 1727).

Q. 60 *How do the Beatitudes call us to moral choices?*
The Beatitudes call us to moral choices by inviting us to purify our hearts and seek the love of God above all else (CCC 1723).

PART TWO
The Holy Mass

CHAPTER 17

At the Last Supper

"Truly, truly, I say to you, unless you eat the flesh of the Son of man and drink his blood, you have no life in you."

John 6:53

Let us begin by reading chapter six of Saint John's Gospel.

Jesus shocked many of his followers by saying that he would give them his Body to eat and his Blood to drink, and that they would not have life in them unless they accepted it. At this many of his followers left him. Peter answered for those who remained faithful. When Jesus asked them, "Will you also go away?" Peter said, "Lord, to whom shall we go? You have the words of eternal life" (Jn 6:67–68).

Peter and the faithful disciples did not foresee how Jesus was going to do what he said; they did not have the slightest idea how it could be possible. But they had come to know and love Jesus; they had come to hunger for the words of eternal life that came from him; and they believed.

Just before he told them this, Jesus had demonstrated his power by feeding a crowd of about five thousand people with a few loaves and fish, and he had announced greater things to come. But he did not explain. When the time came for him to leave his Apostles, Jesus gave them a treasure of immeasurable richness—his own Self in the **Eucharist**. With the utmost simplicity he found a way to give them his Body and Blood to eat and drink:

he changed bread into his Body and wine into his Blood.

This wonderful event took place at Jesus' **Last Supper** with his Apostles the night before he died. They were celebrating one of the great festivals of the Jewish people, the Passover. With Jesus' action the sacrifice of the Old Covenant was ended and the sacrifice of the New Covenant established.

The Passover

The **Passover** commemorated God's rescue of his chosen people from slavery in Egypt. He worked great signs and wonders through his servant Moses to strike the fear of God into the hearts of the Egyptians so that Pharaoh would free the Hebrews and allow them to depart and worship the true God.

Pharaoh was very stubborn about keeping the Hebrews captive until one night the angel of death passed through Egypt, striking down the firstborn sons of the Egyptians.

The Hebrews had been instructed by God through Moses to offer a special sacrifice that night: a spotless lamb, one for each family. Every Hebrew dwelling was to be marked on the doorpost with the blood of the lamb so that the angel of death would pass over without harming those within.

After this event the Egyptians finally let the Hebrews go, for the fear of God had fallen on them.

All of this is important if we are to understand what Jesus did at the Last Supper. We can see the slavery of the Hebrew people as an image of the slavery of all people to sin. And just as God freed the Hebrews, he frees us. The sacrifice that frees man from sin is the Crucifixion and death of our Lord Jesus Christ. He is the Passover Lamb.

Each year the Hebrew people observed the anniversary of the Passover—and the mighty events that led to their freedom—with a special meal. Each family would offer a Paschal lamb in sacrifice and would eat it with unleavened bread and bitter herbs. These were symbols that recalled the original Passover. To this day the Jewish people observe the Passover.

Jesus and his Apostles were celebrating this special meal when Jesus "took bread, and blessed, and broke it, and gave it to the disciples and said, 'Take, eat; this is my body.' And he took a chalice, and when he had given thanks he gave it to them, saying, 'Drink of it, all of you; for this is my blood of the covenant, which is poured out for many for the forgiveness of sins' " (Mt 26:26–28).

The Perfect Sacrifice

From the time of Adam's Fall, men have felt the need to make a public offering to God to make up for their sins and ask for mercy. The firstfruits of a harvest, a lamb or a goat—something needed for life—would be offered on an altar by a priest to indicate that, like everything that exists, they belong to God. Men desired to be restored to that friendship with God which sin had broken. Their sacrifices were an attempt to do this.

Offering a sacrifice has four distinct purposes: to adore God, to thank him, to make up for sin, and to ask his help.

Before the coming of Christ a great many sacrifices were offered to God, but not one of them offered a **victim** that could atone for men's sins. Alone, men were unable to offer to God anything so fitting and precious that it could make up for such a grave offense against God. But God loves us so much and so much desired our reconciliation to him that he gave us an acceptable victim that would satisfy our debt.

Jesus, given to us by the Father, was that acceptable victim. This divine victim was sacrificed upon the Cross to make peace between heaven and earth once and for all.

The word **oblation** is used to indicate the total offering of a victim or gift in a sacrifice. In the oblation of Jesus Christ, he was both priest and victim. For he was held on the Cross by his love alone; at any moment he could have come down from the Cross, but he would not. He truly offered himself. To all appearances he died like a criminal, but, unlike anyone else who was ever crucified, he freely laid down his life and offered himself for the sins of the world.

Being God and Man

When Jesus took the bread at the Last Supper and said, "This is my Body," he made himself present on the table as the gift of the sacrifice. He stood over the gift and looked down upon it, but the gift was no longer bread; it was his Body, it was himself. He did the same thing with the wine; it became his Precious Blood. Jesus could do this because he was God as well as man.

At the Last Supper, the Apostles received the first Holy Communion, and each Apostle received Jesus complete and entire—not part of Jesus but the whole Jesus—Body, Blood, Soul, and Divinity, God and man. The whole Jesus went to Andrew, to Peter, to John, to Philip, to each one. And so he comes to us, too, when we receive Holy Communion. The Apostles were united with Christ and filled with grace. So are we.

But what did the Apostles see when Jesus said, "This is my Body. . . . This is my Blood"? What they saw still looked like bread and wine. What had been bread still had the same weight, color, and taste; what had been wine still had the same taste, odor, and color. But its *substance*, the underlying reality which makes it what it is, had been changed. The looks and other properties known by the senses are called the *appearances*; the Body and Blood of Jesus kept the *appearances* of bread and wine. The **mystery** of this change in the bread and wine is called "**transubstantiation**," which means change of substance.

The substance of bread and wine have been changed into the substance of the Body and Blood of Christ. We cannot see the change but it has happened.

Why does Jesus change bread and wine into his Body and Blood but leave the appearances of bread and wine? The Eucharist is a Sacrament, a sign instituted by Christ to give us grace. The appearances of bread and wine remain as signs that Jesus is true spiritual food and drink for our souls given to us in a special way in the Eucharist. He is the source of our life as Christians.

We call Jesus' presence in the Eucharist the Real Presence. It is called "real" because Jesus is really and truly with us. The Eucharist is no mere symbol of Jesus; it truly is Jesus, under the appearances of bread and wine.

The Everlasting Sacrifice

After the Apostles had each received Holy Communion, Jesus said to them, "Do this in remembrance of me" (Lk 22:19). When he said this he made them priests; for by telling them to do what he had just done—to change bread and wine into his Body and Blood—he gave them the power to do it.

The greatest power of the priesthood is the power to offer this sacrifice of Jesus' Body and Blood. It is the same sacrifice that Jesus offered at the Last Supper and the next day on the Cross. Through this power the Body and Blood of Jesus continue to be offered to God under the appearances of bread and wine whenever the Mass is celebrated.

So God left us an everlasting sacrifice of such richness and power that nothing else can be compared to it.

The Apostles used their powers to feed the new Church of Christ with the Bread from heaven: the Eucharist. They shared their power with other men, co-workers and their successors, so that the Church could continue from generation to generation to offer the great sacrifice, making it present to all who seek it, until the end of time.

Words to Know:
Eucharist   Last Supper   Passover   victim   oblation   mystery   transubstantiation

---

Q. 61   *What is the Eucharist?*

The Eucharist is the Sacrament of the Body, Blood, Soul, and Divinity of Christ, really and truly present under the appearances of bread and wine (CCC 1333).

Q. 62   *What does it mean to say that the whole Christ is contained in the Eucharist under the appearances of bread and wine?*

To say that the whole Christ is contained in the Eucharist under the appearances of bread and wine means that the Body, Blood, Soul, and Divinity of Jesus are present (CCC 1374).

Q. 63   *When did Jesus Christ institute the Eucharist?*

Jesus Christ instituted the Eucharist at the Last Supper when he changed bread and wine into his Body and Blood and commanded the Apostles to do the same in his memory (CCC 1323, 1337).

Q. 64   *Why did Jesus Christ institute the Eucharist?*

Jesus Christ instituted the Eucharist in order to leave his Church a visible sacrifice by which the Sacrifice of the Cross would be re-presented and recalled. In the Eucharist, the benefits of the Cross are applied and spiritual food is given to our souls in Holy Communion (CCC 1366, 1382).

Q. 65   *What is a sacrifice?*

A sacrifice is the public offering of something to God in order to profess that he is Creator and Supreme Ruler to whom everything belongs (CCC 1366, 2099).

CHAPTER 18

The Living Sacrifice

"... for then he would have had to suffer repeatedly since the foundation of the world. But as it is, he has appeared once for all at the end of the age to put away sin by the sacrifice of himself."

Hebrews 9:26

Jesus Christ, through whom all good things come to us, died on Calvary and rose again from the dead. His sacrifice redeemed the human race. Every day that sacrifice is renewed in the Holy Mass. That is what the Mass is all about. The Mass is the same sacrifice as the sacrifice at Calvary; it not only recalls that sacrifice but continues it.

Jesus gave us the precious **Sacrament** of the Eucharist for two reasons: so that we might have eternal life and so that we might have an acceptable sacrifice to offer continually to the Father.

As Catholic writer Frank Sheed expressed it, "The Mass *is* Calvary, as Christ now offers it to his Father." The victim offered is the same —Jesus himself. He is present as he made himself present under the appearances of bread and wine at the Last Supper. The priest is one and the same; for the priest at our altar acts in the person of Jesus to change the bread and wine into the Body and Blood of the Lord.

On the altar Jesus offers himself through the words and actions of the priest, without shedding his blood or dying again. After his resurrection Jesus can no longer die. But he still offers his one sacrifice on the Cross to the Father for us. The Bible tells us that he is doing that right now in heaven, as our high priest there (Heb 7:24–25; 8:1–2; 9:11–14). At the

Mass, Jesus makes the heavenly offering of his Body and Blood present on earth, under the appearances of bread and wine. We join with the priest and each other to offer Jesus to the Father, as well as offering ourselves to him with Jesus. In this way, we grow more deeply as the Church, the Body of Christ on earth.

A Memorial

A memorial is a recalling of a past event. Besides being a sacrifice, the Mass is a **memorial** by which until the end of time we call to mind the death of Christ. Christ said to his Apostles, "Do this in memory of me."

He did not mean, however, that the Mass would be *only* a memorial. In the Mass we not only remember Christ's death on the Cross, but Christ brings his sacrifice before us in a real and sacramental way.

Mass is a memorial of Christ's Resurrection as well. The Church teaches that it is "a memorial of his death and Resurrection." Here, too, the reality is more than a recollection. For the chief priest at Mass is the Risen Christ who is present in the Eucharist.

The Four Ends of the Mass

Holy Mass is the perfect prayer. So it has the same ends, or purposes, as prayer.

1. The Mass is an act of supreme worship; it is Christ's greatest gift to his Church. Men with nothing worthy to offer God have now been given a victim and a sacrifice of infinite value: Jesus Christ himself.

2. The Mass is a prayer of thanksgiving; the word "eucharist" actually means "thanksgiving." We have so much to thank God for: our lives, with all that they contain of family and friends, people, places, and things. Most of all, there is the supernatural life of grace given to us by Jesus Christ, our Savior. It is through the life of grace that we have hope of reaching heaven and can enjoy great happiness even now.

Through the Mass we have the chance to thank God for all his benefits, most of all for his generosity and mercy in sending us Jesus, his Son. And it is Jesus, his gift to us, whom we now offer back to him. God is infinitely pleased with this gift that he has put in our hands.

3. The Mass is a way to **make satisfaction for** (make up for) sins. We pray: "Lamb of God, you take away the sins of the world, have mercy on us . . . grant us peace."

Are we asking Jesus to do something that he has already done? Are we asking him to take away the sins of the world again and again, every time the Mass is offered?

No; there is really only one Mass, and it was offered on Calvary once for all. And it is this one sacrifice that is offered on all our altars at Mass. Through the gift of the Holy Eucharist, Jesus has extended his sacrifice in time and space. Our participation at Mass is our time to be with Christ at the Cross.

4. The Mass is our best means of petitioning the Father and obtaining the graces we ask for, both for ourselves and for others. In the Mass we are offering to God the perfect sacrifice, Jesus Christ, the most pleasing offering we have to give, and God will be pleased by our offering so great a gift.

Words to Know:

Sacrament   memorial
make satisfaction for

Q. 66   *What is the Holy Mass?*
The Holy Mass is the sacrifice of the Body and Blood of Jesus Christ. This sacrifice is offered to God under the appearances of bread and wine through the ministry of a priest, in order to remember, renew, and re-present the Sacrifice of the Cross, and to be received in the sacred meal of Holy Communion (CCC 1367, 1382).

Q. 67   *Is the Sacrifice of the Mass the same as the Sacrifice of the Cross?*
The Sacrifice of the Mass is the same sacrifice as the Sacrifice of the Cross; the only difference is in the manner of offering it (CCC 1364, 1367).

Q. 68   *Who is the priest and the victim in the Holy Sacrifice of the Mass?*
In the Holy Sacrifice of the Mass Jesus Christ is the priest, acting through his ordained minister, and Christ is the victim, offered to the Father under the appearances of bread and wine (CCC 1367).

Q. 69   *What is the difference between the Sacrifice of the Cross and the Sacrifice of the Mass?*
On the Cross, Christ shed his blood and died; in the Mass, he offers himself under the appearances of bread and wine by the ministry of a priest, in an unbloody manner and without dying; on the Cross he merited redemption for man; in the Mass, he applies the benefits of his sacrifice on the Cross (CCC 1367).

Q. 70   *Why is the Mass offered to God?*
The Mass is offered to God to give him the supreme worship of adoration; to thank him for his blessings to us; to make satisfaction for our sins; and to obtain graces for the good of the faithful, living and dead (CCC 1365, 1368).

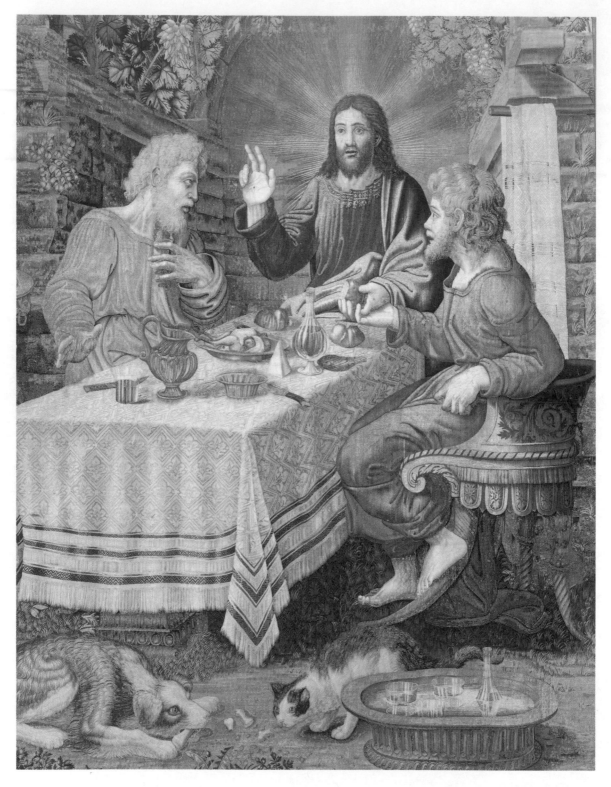

The Feast of God

"For as often as you eat this bread and drink the chalice, you proclaim the Lord's death until he comes."

1 Corinthians 11:26

At Mass we celebrate the death and Resurrection of the Lord in a sacred banquet. These are truly matters for celebration. We should take time out for special activities to underline the significance of our redemption and to rejoice with our risen Lord.

However, this is no ordinary, casual celebration like a birthday party or a big family meal. This is a sacred celebration; it is *holy*. It is time consecrated to God, dedicated to him, and set aside for him alone. Therefore we should approach this celebration with an attitude of reverence and profound respect. We express reverence by our attitude and our actions: by proper dress, by silence, by genuflection, by prayerfulness. When we understand this, we are ready to consider Holy Mass as a celebration. The mysteries we celebrate are worthy of the deepest awe. With Jesus, as with anyone whom we love, friendship and respect must go together. But Jesus is more than just a friend; he is God. We must never forget who he is and who we are; he is the Creator, and we are his creatures.

Sacred Banquet

What is the special activity which makes the Mass a celebration? It is the sacred banquet, the holy meal—Communion. A common meal has always been a way of celebrating important occasions.

A big family meal is a good example of a celebration. We show that the cause for celebration is important to us, not only as individuals but as a family, a group, and a community. It is important enough, in fact, to take a group of individuals, each of whom could have gone his own way, and bring them together in a unifying action. Why do we all do something together? Because it is important to us. Those who participate become part of something greater than any one person.

Table of the Lord

We have seen that the Mass is the re-presentation of Christ's sacrifice on Calvary. We have watched and prayed with the priest. We now have the wonderful opportunity to go to Holy Communion, to receive Christ in the Eucharist, the Word made flesh.

In Old Testament sacrifices, the people offered God a gift, such as a lamb. The lamb was slaughtered to offer it up. But this was not all. To complete the religious ritual or celebration of the sacrifice, the people would eat the lamb. The gift that they offered was received back as a gift. The people were trying to be in closer union with God by partaking of something that had been offered to and accepted by God.

As we have seen, the Mass is a sacrifice far greater than any other. It is the one and only perfect sacrifice because it is the sacrifice of Jesus himself. But here, too, the religious ritual is not really complete until we partake of the gift that has been offered.

We join the priest in offering Jesus to the Father; the Father accepts our gift and gives it back to us to eat. Therefore, the Mass is considered a feast, a meal, and a sacred banquet. It can be thought of as a big family meal as long as two points are kept in mind: the family consists of all those joined in the Church of Christ, and the food is the sacred Body and Blood of Christ. Holy Communion is normally meant to be received in the communal religious service which is the Mass.

We are to go forward as God's family—not alone but in company.

In the Our Father, we pray for our "daily bread," expressing our trust in God who provides for all our earthly needs. On another level, our "daily bread" is Christ, the spiritual bread in the Eucharistic banquet that we need in order to be made holy.

And we pray to "our" Father, not just "my" Father, because we are meant to grow into the perfect unity of a happy and glorious community—a family—in the Mystical Body of Christ.

In the sacred meal of Holy Mass, we come together as God's People to receive the Body of Christ in the Eucharist. As we do, we are spiritually fed by Jesus to be more truly his Body in the world.

O Sacred Banquet,
in which Christ is received,
the memory of his Passion is renewed,
the mind is filled with grace,
and a pledge of future glory is given us.
Alleluia.

Q. 71   *How is the Mass a sacrifice and a meal?*
The Mass is a sacrifice because, on the altar, Jesus is offered to the Father in an unbloody re-presentation of the Sacrifice of the Cross. It is a meal because we are invited to receive Jesus, who has offered himself for us (CCC 1382).

Q. 72   *How can we most perfectly participate in the Mass?*
We can most perfectly participate in the Mass by listening to and meditating upon the Word of God, uniting ourselves in the sacrifice of Christ offered to the Father, and worthily receiving Holy Communion (CCC1388–89)

Q. 73   *Is the same Jesus Christ, who was born of the Blessed Virgin Mary, truly present in the Eucharist?*
Yes, the same Jesus Christ, who was born of the Blessed Virgin Mary, is truly present in the Eucharist (CCC 1373).

Q. 74   *How is the Eucharist food for our souls?*
Just as normal food preserves and renews the body, the Eucharist preserves, renews, and increases the soul's life of grace we received at Baptism (CCC 1392).

Q. 75   *How does the Eucharist unite us in Christ?*
The Eucharist unites us in Christ by bringing all of the faithful into one body: the Mystical Body of Christ (CCC 1396).

CHAPTER 20

Promise and Fulfillment

"I am the living bread which came down from heaven; if any one eats of this bread, he will live for ever; and the bread which I shall give for the life of the world is my flesh."

John 6:51

In Saint John's Gospel we read the text,

"This is a hard saying" (Jn 6:60).

These were the words with which many of his followers greeted Jesus' announcement of the Holy Eucharist. If Jesus had been misunderstood he could have set things straight before they walked away from him. But Jesus did not stop them. In fact, the Gospel says: "But Jesus, knowing in himself that his disciples murmured at it, said to them, 'Do you take offense at this?'" (Jn 6:61). The Gospel goes on to say: "After this many of his disciples drew back and no longer walked with him" (Jn 6:66).

What had Jesus said, exactly, which they would not accept?

[H]e who eats my flesh and drinks my blood has eternal life, and I will raise him up at the last day. For my flesh is food indeed, and my blood is drink indeed (Jn 6:54–55).

And what did those who did not believe say?

"How can this man give us his flesh to eat?" (Jn 6:52).

We Have Come To Believe

The Gospel goes on to tell us:

Jesus said to the Twelve, "Will you also go away?" Simon Peter answered him, "Lord, to whom shall we go? You have the words of eternal life; and we have believed, and have come to know, that you are the Holy One of God" (Jn 6:67–69).

Jesus had not led his followers to this point to catch them unprepared. As Peter put it, they had "believed and come to know."

The Apostles believed not because they fully understood, but because they had faith in Jesus. This is what Jesus was looking for. The Gospel says: "Then they said to him, 'What must we do, to be doing the works of God?' Jesus answered them, 'This is the work of God, that you believe in him whom he has sent'" (Jn 6:28–29). Jesus had given them more than sufficient evidence to believe in him. He had been going about doing good, teaching and preaching the Good News of the Kingdom of God, and performing many miracles.

In every generation Jesus looks for generous people who really hear him, who really want to be his followers and really put their faith in him, who will not turn away because of the "hard saying" about the Eucharist, who will say with Saint Peter: "You have the words of eternal life; and we have believed, and have come to know, that you are the Holy One of God" (Jn 6:68–69).

My Flesh Is Food Indeed

Just what was Christ offering the crowds when he announced the Eucharist? He said that his "Flesh is food indeed" and his "Blood is real drink." We have seen that he meant this to be taken literally. However, he did not mean that the Eucharist would be food for our bodies. The Eucharist is spiritual food, nourishment for our souls, which comes to us through our bodies.

What happens when we receive the Eucharist worthily? Because the Eucharist truly is the Body and Blood of Jesus, it is the source of all grace. It can transform us by the increase of sanctifying grace, which is God's life in the soul. We grow in holiness, which means that we become more like Jesus. Receiving the Eucharist worthily pardons our venial sins. Because it is such "rich and nourishing" food for our souls, it cancels out our lesser failings. It also strengthens us to overcome temptations and helps us to break bad habits.

Christ has a plan for extending his Kingdom to the whole world: he offers his followers the invitation to become other Christs. Those who feed on his Body and Blood have life in him—Christ's life, which does not destroy our personality, but perfects, enriches, and preserves it to life everlasting.

"I am the living bread which came down from heaven; if any one eats of this bread, he will live for ever."

John 6:51

Q. 76 *Why do you believe that Jesus Christ is truly present in the Eucharist?*

I believe that Jesus Christ is truly present in the Eucharist because he himself said that he would give us his Body to eat and his Blood to drink. At the Last Supper, he consecrated bread and wine and made them his Body and Blood, and commanded the Church to "Do this in memory of me" (CCC 1375).

Q. 77 *What effect does the Eucharist have on one who receives it worthily?*

In one who receives it worthily, the Holy Eucharist preserves and increases grace, which is the life of the soul. The Holy Eucharist takes away venial sin and strengthens us against mortal sin, and it gives spiritual joy and consolation by increasing charity and the hope of eternal life, of which it is the pledge (CCC 1392, 1394, 1402).

Q. 78 *How do we receive the Eucharist worthily?*

To receive the Eucharist worthily, we must be in a state of grace, we must recognize whom we are receiving in Communion, and we must participate in the Eucharistic fast (CCC 1385, 1387).

CHAPTER 21

New Life

"Jesus said to her, 'I am the resurrection and the life; he who believes in me, though he die, yet shall he live, and whoever lives and believes in me shall never die. Do you believe this?'"

John 11:25–26

When Jesus died, his disciples, helped by Joseph of Arimathea, came and took his body and buried it in a tomb cut in rock in a garden. This was done in haste, because they had to prepare for the Sabbath (Lk 23:54).

What would happen next? Was it all over, the glorious dream, the visible evidence of the power of God? The Messiah was dead, their beloved Jesus. The Apostles were in hiding for fear of the Jewish leaders.

Then, on the first day of the week, some of the women who had travelled with Jesus and the Apostles set out for the tomb with spices to anoint the body of Jesus and to tend to the details of ceremonial burial which had not been observed the day he died. On the way they began to wonder who would open the tomb for them, since a great stone had been rolled into place to seal it.

But when they got there the stone had been rolled back and an angel from heaven was sitting on it. He informed them that Jesus, who had been crucified, had risen from the dead. He invited them into the tomb to see for themselves.

The women looked in and saw that the tomb was empty. Then the angel said: "Go quickly and tell his disciples that he has risen from the dead, and behold, he is going before you to Galilee; there you will see him" (Mt 28:7).

The women hurried back to the Apostles, filled with awe and great joy. But the Apostles did not believe their marvelous news. Peter and John set out to see for themselves; they found the empty tomb with nothing in it but the wrappings in which Jesus had been buried (Jn 20:6–7).

When the Apostles were gathered together Jesus suddenly appeared among them. "Peace be with you," he said.

The Apostles were in a panic, thinking they were seeing a ghost. Jesus reassured them, telling them that it was really he. He invited them to touch his flesh and asked for something to eat. They gave him a piece of cooked fish and he ate it to show that he was not a ghost (Lk 24:36–43).

In these and other ways Jesus helped them realize that he had risen from the dead and that he was really standing there before them. How they rejoiced!

Then Jesus breathed on them, strengthening them with the Holy Spirit and giving them the power to forgive sins: "Receive the Holy Spirit. If you forgive the sins of any, they are forgiven; if you retain the sins of any, they are

retained" (Jn 20:22–23). He told them that they were to be his witnesses to all nations, beginning at Jerusalem (Lk 24:47).

After that, Jesus did not remain with them, but he appeared to them on several occasions, putting the finishing touches to his work on earth. During one of his appearances by the Sea of Galilee, Jesus asked Peter. "Simon, son of John, do you love me more than these?" Peter answered "Yes, Lord; you know that I love you." Jesus said to him, "Feed my lambs." A second time he said to him, "Simon, son of John, do you love me?" Peter answered "Yes, Lord; you know that I love you." Jesus said to him, "Tend my sheep." Jesus said to Peter the third time, "Simon, son of John, do you love me?" Peter was grieved because he said to him the third time, "Do you love me?" And Peter said to him, "Lord, you know everything; you know that I love you" (Jn 21:15–17).

Jesus was giving Peter a chance to declare his love three times before witnesses because Peter had denied Jesus three times before witnesses when Jesus was on trial.

When Peter had answered his questions, Jesus instructed him, "Feed my lambs; feed my sheep." There Jesus made Peter the universal shepherd of all his followers, the first Pope. At last Jesus simply said to Peter: "Follow me" (Jn 21:19).

Forty days after his Resurrection, Jesus ascended to heaven in the presence of his followers. Before this he had instructed the Apostles not to go anywhere until he sent them the Holy Spirit, who would lead them in all truth and give them special power to extend Christ's Church to every part of the earth. He promised to remain with his Church always, even to the end of the world (Mt 28:20).

What happened next is recorded in the book of the Bible called the Acts of the Apostles. It tells of the coming of the Holy Spirit in the form of tongues of fire, of the conversion of Saint Paul and the works of the Apostles, and of the wonderful early days of the Church and the first Christian communities.

Resurrected Life

When Jesus rose from the dead on Easter Sunday he proved that he was truly the Son of God, as he had said. This meant that his death had not been in vain. He really had redeemed the world from sin. It also meant that the powers that he had given his Apostles were real, and so were his promises to send the Holy Spirit and to remain always with his Church.

But Jesus did more than just pay for our sins by his death on Calvary. His Resurrection on Easter Sunday was a sign that he had also brought us new life. This new life is the life of sanctifying grace, God's own life within us, which enables us to desire and to do what God wants and what will truly make us happy.

Jesus' Resurrection is also a sign of hope that we too will one day rise from the dead just as he did.

Q. 79 *After his death, what did Jesus Christ do?*

After his death, Jesus Christ descended into hell to take the souls of the just who had died before that time into paradise. Then he rose from the dead, taking up his body which had been buried (CCC 632, 638).

Q. 80 *What did Jesus Christ do after his Resurrection?*

After his Resurrection, Jesus Christ remained on earth forty days and taught his Apostles all they needed to know to continue his ministry through the Church. Then he ascended to heaven, where he sits at the right hand of God the Father almighty (CCC 642, 659).

Q. 81 *Why did Jesus Christ remain on earth forty days after his Resurrection?*

Jesus Christ remained on earth forty days after his Resurrection in order to show that he had truly risen from the dead, to confirm his disciples' faith in him, and to instruct them more profoundly in his teaching (CCC 642, 659).

Q. 82 *What is the significance of the Resurrection?*

The Resurrection proves that Jesus is God, and that all he taught and promised, including our share in the Resurrection, is true (CCC 651, 653–54).

"I am the resurrection and the life. . . ."
John 11:25

Come into the Lord's Presence Singing for Joy

"And one called to another and said: 'Holy, holy, holy is the Lord of hosts; the whole earth is full of his glory.'"

Isaiah 6:3

We have been studying the death and Resurrection of our Lord Jesus Christ by which he redeemed all mankind. We have seen that the Mass is the re-presentation of this saving sacrifice. We have seen that through his ordained priest, Christ himself presides over every Mass. Now we will look at each part of the Mass.

We should approach not only Mass but the church building itself with the proper attitude. This means getting ready to take part in public worship of God. We get ready outwardly by wearing suitable clothes. We get ready inwardly by understanding our purpose in coming: to offer the Holy Sacrifice of the Mass with the priest and to be nourished by the Word of God and the precious Body and Blood of our Lord Jesus Christ. We will come eagerly if we have thought deeply about the meaning of all these things.

The Sacred Liturgy

The public worship of God is called the Sacred Liturgy. The word **liturgy** means "work of the people." It includes the worship we offer to God when we come together as his people, the Body of Christ, especially in the Mass. Through the Sacred Liturgy, we on earth take part in the worship of God that goes on in heaven with the angels and the saints.

The main parts of the Mass are the Liturgy of the Word and the Liturgy of the Eucharist. But before these two parts comes a smaller part called the Introductory Rites. The Introductory Rites prepare us to take part worthily and to focus our hearts and our minds on the Mass.

First there is the *Entrance Antiphon* or *Hymn* during which the priest and altar servers enter the church and go to the altar. It is accompanied by signs of reverence, such as the carrying of candles, incense, and the Book of the Gospels.

After the entrance song, the priest and the people make the Sign of the Cross. The priest greets the people: "The Lord be with you;" and the people answer: "And with your spirit."

Next is the *Penitential Rite*. The priest invites the people to think of their sins and be sorry for them. Then we all acknowledge our sins together, using one of three possible prayers of confession. This is not the same thing as the Sacrament of Penance, but it helps to purify our hearts.

The prayer of confession usually used is called the *Confiteor*. It begins: "I confess to almighty God and to you, my brothers and sisters . . . ," and it is followed by the invocations: "Lord, have mercy. Christ, have mercy. Lord, have mercy." Or "Kyrie, eleison. Christe, eleison. Kyrie, eleison."

The Penitential Rite reminds us that we are sinners in need of God's mercy. It reminds us

that we are all in desperate need of God's forgiveness. Put another way, we must remember that almighty God is almighty God and that we are merely his creatures in need of forgiveness. Then we begin to see things in the right perspective.

After asking for forgiveness we are ready to praise God and to recall that his divine Son became man to redeem us from our sins and make us children of his heavenly Father. We do so in the *Gloria*, a prayer that was once a Christmas hymn and begins with the words with which the angels greeted the shepherds: "Glory to God in the highest, and on earth peace to people of good will" (see Lk 2:14). The Gloria is used at most Sunday Masses and on other special days.

In this prayer we offer God praise, honor, and adoration, addressing Father, Son, and Holy Spirit. We plead with the God-man Jesus Christ to hear our prayers and ask him to give us a share in his sacrifice and his victory over death as they are re-presented in the Mass.

The Introductory Rites are ended with the *Opening Prayer* or *Collect*. The priest invites the people to pray, and together they may spend some moments in silence so that they can realize that they are in God's presence and make their petitions. Then the priest says the prayer that expresses the theme of the particular Mass, whether it be, for example, a Sunday, the feast day of a saint, or a feast of the Blessed Virgin.

These prayers are determined by the day of the liturgical year. The liturgical year is the Church's calendar; it has its own seasons and special feast days. We know about Advent and Lent, the two penitential seasons, and there are other seasons in the liturgical year. The seasons are to remind us of the life and teachings of Jesus and to help us live as he wants us to.

Not only are certain prayers and the readings of the Mass determined by the liturgical season; so are the church decorations and the priest's vestments. The color of the vestment is an indication of what season or feast day is being celebrated.

Word to Know:

     liturgy

> **Introductory Rites**
>
> **Entrance Antiphon (Hymn)**
> **Greeting of the People**
> **Penitential Rite**
> **Gloria**
> **Opening Prayer (Collect)**

Q. 83   *Who presides over every Mass?*
        Christ himself, through his ordained priest, presides over every Mass (CCC 1348).

Q. 84   *What are the two main parts of the Mass?*
        The two main parts of the Mass are the Liturgy of the Word and the Liturgy of the Eucharist (CCC 1346).

"Then I will go to the altar of God, to God my exceeding joy; and I will praise you with the lyre, O God, my God."

Psalm 43:4

99

Speak Lord, Your Servant Is Listening

"We are of God. Whoever knows God listens to us, and he who is not of God does not listen to us. By this we know the spirit of truth and the spirit of error."

1 John 4:6

As we have seen, the Introductory Rites involve our speaking to God. We pray for God's forgiveness in the Penitential Rite, praise his goodness in the Gloria, and pray the Opening Prayer or Collect. In the next part of the Mass, the LITURGY OF THE WORD, God speaks to us.

At Sunday Mass there are three readings from the Bible. The *First Reading* is usually from the Old Testament. (During the Easter season it is from the Acts of the Apostles.) From the Old Testament we learn the history of creation and of God's chosen people, the Hebrews. Sometimes we hear prophecies of the coming of the Savior. And many Old Testament events foreshadow the Gospel. For example, the Passover lamb foretells, or prefigures, Jesus' sacrifice on the Cross and the Holy Eucharist.

The First Reading is followed by the *Responsorial Psalm*, the reading or singing of a Psalm with a refrain that we repeat. The Psalms express every kind of prayer: praise, thanksgiving, reparation for sin, and petition.

The *Second Reading* comes from the Epistles (letters) that the Apostles wrote to the first Christian Churches. Some of the letters explained what to do with collection money or how to deal with troublemakers. For the most part, the letters discuss how to grow in holiness, how to pray, and how to treat the people around us with true Christian charity.

Next we stand for the *Gospel*, to show our reverence for the words of Jesus. After we recite or sing the Alleluia verse, the priest says: "The Lord be with you." The people answer: "And with your spirit." The priest goes on to say: "A reading from the holy Gospel according to Matthew" (or Mark, Luke, or John). Then the priest makes the Sign of the Cross on the Lectionary (or the book of the Gospels), and then on his forehead, lips, and heart. The people do the same as they answer: "Glory to you, Lord." The little crosses indicate that the word of our Lord is to be in our thoughts, on our lips, and in our hearts.

We hear the Gospel readings again and again, and we may be quite familiar with them. Why go over them so many times?

The Gospels are the record of what Jesus said and did on earth. Listening again and again to the teachings of Jesus or the stories about his miracles is a way to spend time with him, to know and love him better. The more we think about Jesus' life and words, the more we learn about him. We can never go over the Gospels too many times; for every word and action is the word and action of God himself as he lived and walked among men.

We must pay attention during the readings. We must try not to drift off into daydreams during a familiar reading. God gives us special graces if we listen when he speaks to us.

In fact, we share the privilege of the disciples, to whom Jesus said: "Blessed are the eyes which see what you see! For I tell you that many prophets and kings desired to see what you see, and did not see it, and to hear what you hear, and did not hear it" (Lk 10:23–24).

Our Lord was talking about his own words and actions. He included in this privilege not only those who lived with him but all the people down through the ages who would do their best to get to know him by studying the accounts of his life, guided by the teaching and Tradition of the Church.

Next comes the *Homily*. The readings and Psalm we have heard have been chosen to illustrate a theme. This theme may be explained by the priest in his homily. Jesus' words and actions, which are sometimes hard to understand, are explained in light of the Church's teaching. The priest may talk about how we can apply what Jesus said and did to our own lives, and how understanding the Gospel can help us decide how to think and act.

At Sunday Mass, and on Holy Days or solemn (special) feasts, the sermon, or homily, is followed by the *Creed*, recited by everyone together. The Creed is a statement of what all

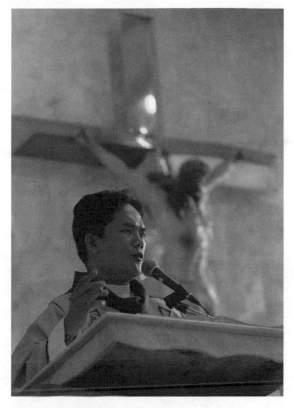

Catholics believe. We have listened to Sacred Scripture, and the priest has explained it and applied it to practical cases; now it is time to express our faith in what God has revealed and taught us. In reciting the Creed, we testify that we believe what God has revealed to men. We worship God, the author of all truth, with our minds.

The Creed is followed by the *General Intercessions* or *Prayers of the Faithful*. These prayers are for the needs of the Church, for our public authorities, for the salvation of the world, for those oppressed by any need, and for our local community and families.

This concludes the Liturgy of the Word.

"Man shall not live by bread alone, but by every word that proceeds from the mouth of God."

Matthew 4:4

"Speak, for your servant hears."

1 Samuel 3:10

Liturgy of the Word

First Reading
Responsorial Psalm
Second Reading
Gospel
Homily
Profession of Faith (Creed)
Prayers of the Faithful

Q. 85   *What does the Liturgy of the Word include?*
The Liturgy of the Word includes readings from the Old Testament, Psalms, Epistles, and the Gospel, a homily, the profession of faith, and the Prayers of the Faithful (CCC 1349).

Q. 86   *What is the homily?*
The homily is an exhortation to accept the Word of God proclaimed in the readings, and to put the Word of God into practice (CCC 1349).

Lift Up the Cup of Salvation

"When he was at table with them, he took the bread and blessed and broke it, and gave it to them. And their eyes were opened and they recognized him; and he vanished out of their sight."

Luke 24:30–31

The LITURGY OF THE EUCHARIST begins with the *Preparation of the Gifts*. Bread and wine are brought up to the priest from the people. The priest accepts them, places them on the altar, and with special prayers offers them to God.

All of the words and actions are rich with meaning. Whenever God wants to do something for us, he always does it in a way that helps our understanding; he uses a sign on one level that shows us what is happening on a higher level.

The bread and wine brought forward from the people will soon become the Body and Blood of Jesus. The bread is made up of many grains of wheat and the wine of many grapes, just as the people, though many, are made into the one Body of Christ through the mysteries of the Eucharist. We, though many, share the one Bread and are made one.

The grapes were crushed in order to become wine, and the wheat was ground into flour to make bread. When we think of this, we can remember that we must die to ourselves, to our sins and faults, and live a new life in Christ.

At this time in the Mass we should be offering ourselves to God: our whole selves, including our joys and sorrows. A hymn may be sung that can help us understand the actions and the signs.

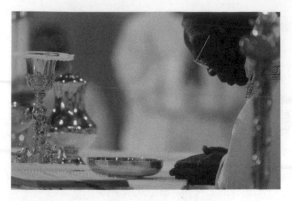

The prayers during the Preparation of the Gifts acknowledge God's goodness as Lord of all creation and the goodness of creation itself. They ask God's blessing on these gifts which are to become for us the Bread of Life and our spiritual drink. After the priest offers the bread, and again after he offers the wine, the people respond, "Blessed be God for ever."

The *Washing of the Hands* of the priest signifies the great purity with which we should approach the Eucharist. It is a prayer to God to wash away our sins as we come close to him.

The priest then invites the people to pray that our sacrifice may be accepted by God, the almighty Father.

The people respond with a prayer that our sacrifice may be accepted at the hands of the priest for three purposes: 1. the praise and glory of God's name; 2. for our benefit; and 3. the good of all the Church. This prayer can remind us that in all that we do, God's glory must be considered first; our good and the good of all the Church, though very important, come after. With his hands extended, the priest then says a prayer that the gifts will be acceptable and pleasing to God. The people stand for this prayer and give consent to it by saying, "Amen."

The Eucharistic Prayer

Now comes the high point of the Mass, called the *Eucharistic Prayer* or *Canon*. It is in this part of the Mass that bread and wine become the Body and Blood of our Lord and the sacrifice is offered to God.

The prayer begins with the *Preface*, a consideration of the coming sacrifice in light of the liturgical season of the year or of a feast day. It ends as we join our voices to those of the angels in heaven in the hymn called the *Sanctus*:

"Holy, Holy, Holy Lord God of hosts. Heaven and earth are full of your glory. Hosanna in the highest. Blessed is he who comes in the name of the Lord. Hosanna in the highest."

The word "**hosanna**" (a Hebrew word meaning "save us") is a special exclamation of joy in the salvation God has promised to us. It expresses our joyful expectation of God coming to us as our salvation.

The people, who were standing to give praise, now kneel and remain kneeling for the most solemn part of the Mass.

The priest extends his hands over the gifts and invokes the Holy Spirit, asking him to come upon them and make them holy so that they may become the Body and Blood of our Lord Jesus Christ. Then he continues with the *Consecration*, in which he says: "This is my Body . . . this is the chalice of my Blood." At this moment, the bread and wine become the Body and Blood of Jesus.

The priest holds up the consecrated Host and then the chalice with the Precious Blood; as he holds them up for the people to adore, he and the people offer the Holy Sacrifice, Christ's Body and Blood, to our heavenly Father.

This is the part of the Mass where we are called on to proclaim our belief in this great mystery of our faith—that Jesus really is present on the altar now.

The Eucharistic Prayer also contains prayers

Liturgy of the Eucharist

OFFERTORY

Preparation of the Altar
Preparation of the Gifts
Offering of the Gifts
Washing of the Hands
Prayers over the Gifts

EUCHARISTIC PRAYER
(CANON)

Preface
Sanctus
Prayer of Thanksgiving
Invocation of the Holy Spirit
Consecration
Offering to the Father
Doxology

for the Church, for the living, and for the dead. Then the priest takes the chalice and the paten with the Host and, lifting them up, says:

"Through him, and with him, and in him, O God, almighty Father, in the unity of the Holy Spirit, all glory and honor is yours, for ever and ever."

This prayer is called a **Doxology**. The people respond with "Amen," which means that they fully assent to the prayer of the priest, and the sacrifice is complete.

Words to Know:

hosanna   Doxology

"First of all, then, I urge that supplications, prayers, intercessions, and thanksgivings be made for all men."

1 Timothy 2:1

Q. 87   *When do the bread and wine become the Body and Blood of Jesus?*

By the power of the Holy Spirit, the bread and wine become the Body and Blood of Jesus at the moment of the Consecration when the priest says "This Is My Body" and "This Is My Blood" (CCC 1353, 1376).

Q. 88   *After the Consecration is there anything left of the bread and wine?*

After the Consecration neither the bread nor the wine is present any longer, but there remain only the appearances of bread and wine (CCC 1376).

Q. 89   *What is the change from bread and wine into the Body, Blood, Soul, and Divinity of Jesus called?*

The change from bread and wine into the Body, Blood, Soul, and Divinity of Jesus is called transubstantiation (CCC 1376).

Come to the Table of the Lord

"And they held steadfastly to the apostles' teaching and fellowship, to the breaking of bread and the prayers."

Acts 2:42

The Communion Rite follows the Eucharistic Prayer in the Liturgy of the Eucharist. The sacred victim, accepted by the Father—since it is his own divine Son—is now given back to us as the greatest gift we can receive.

At the conclusion of the Eucharistic Prayer, after the people say "Amen," the priest puts down the chalice and the paten with the Host and says: "At the Savior's command and formed by divine teaching, we dare to say…"

Then we join in the *Our Father* in order to praise God and place our petitions before him. This is the prayer that our Lord himself taught us as the model for all our prayers. It is certainly fitting, as we pause in the action of the

Mass, to reach out to God the Father with these words in which Jesus taught his Apostles to pray simply, with confidence and love.

The Our Father, called the perfect prayer, contains all the spiritual ingredients we need to move us into a close and loving family, the People of God. Jesus taught us to say "our" Father, not "my" Father, because God wishes to live with us in a community. As God has said so many times in the Old Testament: "I will be your God and you will be my people."

My Peace I Give You

Saint Paul, in his letter to the Philippians, speaks of the peace of God "which passes all understanding" (Phil 4:7). This priceless treasure of peace is Christ's gift to us. At the Last Supper, Christ says: "Peace I leave with you; my peace I give to you; not as the world gives do I give to you. Let not your hearts be troubled, neither let them be afraid" (Jn 14:27).

At this point in the Mass, we may offer each other a sign of Christ's peace, the peace of forgiveness and the reassurance of having his mercy and love. To preserve this gift we must seek to live in peace every day with family and friends and everyone we meet.

As the *Rite of Peace* ends, the priest takes the Host and breaks it over the paten. He places a small piece in the chalice, saying quietly: "May this mingling of the Body and Blood of our Lord Jesus Christ bring eternal life to us who receive it."

Meanwhile, everyone prays: "Lamb of God, you take away the sins of the world, have mercy on us . . . grant us peace."

Jesus, of course, is the "Lamb of God;" he takes away the sins of the world. The Paschal lamb that is eaten by Jewish families to celebrate the Passover, which freed the Israelites from the Egyptians, is a symbol of the true Paschal Lamb who frees us from the slavery of our sins.

I Am Not Worthy

Close to Communion now, we repeat the words of a Roman centurion who once asked Jesus to save one of his servants from death. The centurion did not consider himself worthy to receive Jesus. He asked that Jesus simply give the word and his servant would be cured. Jesus marveled at this man's faith and granted his request. Now we, too, say as the centurion did:

> *"Lord, I am not worthy that you should enter under my roof, but only say the word and my soul shall be healed" (see Mt 8:8).*

Then the priest takes Communion, and the *Communion Antiphon* is recited or sung.

Finally we go up to receive Holy Communion. The priest holds the Host before the communicant, and says: "The Body of Christ," to which the communicant answers: "Amen." When we say "Amen" we are saying: "Yes, I

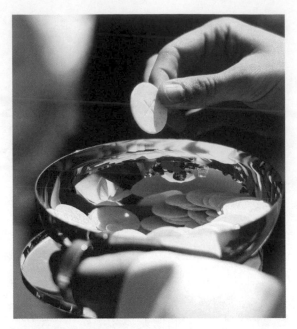

believe that this is really Jesus Christ."

If we are unable to receive Communion for some reason, we should use the time to pray and ask Jesus to be present with us.

Giving Thanks

Receiving Holy Communion allows us to be alone with God in a private way. It is one of the best chances we have to thank Jesus for everything he gives us—especially the gift of his Body and Blood.

There is an incident in the Gospel in which Jesus cures ten lepers. They were cured as they were on their way to show themselves to the priests as Jesus directed. Only one of them returned to Jesus to thank him.

Let's remember to be grateful to Jesus for coming to us in Holy Communion. How do we welcome him? Do we receive him on our tongue or in our hand and then close our minds and hearts to him? Do we at least keep him company for five or ten minutes?

When Communion has been distributed, the priest cleans the paten over the chalice

COMMUNION RITE

The Lord's Prayer (Our Father)
Rite of Peace
Breaking of the Bread
Lamb of God (Agnus Dei)
Communion of the Priest
Communion Antiphon
Communion of the People
Prayer after Communion

CONCLUDING RITE

Blessing
Closing Hymn (Recessional)

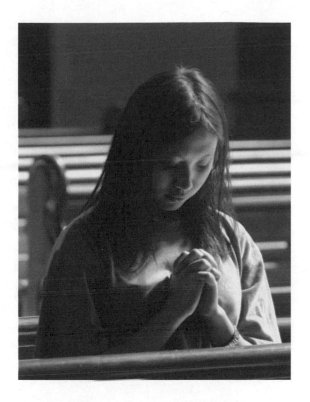

and then cleans the chalice itself. The people have a chance to pray quietly. The priest may sit down for a time to continue the silence and thanksgiving. Then, standing at the chair or at the altar, the priest says the *Prayer after Communion*, which asks that our share in the Eucharist be fruitful.

The *Blessing* in the name of the Blessed Trinity follows, and then the priest declares: "Go forth, the Mass is ended."

The people answer: "Thanks be to God."

There may be a *Closing Hymn (Recessional)* as the priest leaves the altar.

After Mass, we should try to spend some time—however brief—alone with Jesus. We may pray for ourselves; for the Church, the Pope, priests, and religious; for our families, friends, and others. A prayer book with a selection of prayers for thanksgiving after Communion may be helpful.

Q. 90 *Who is the Lamb of God?*

Jesus is the Lamb of God, whose sacrifice takes away the sin of the world (CCC 608).

Q. 91 *When the Host is broken into several parts, is the Body of Jesus Christ broken?*

When the Host is broken into several parts, the Body of Jesus Christ is not broken, but only the appearances of the bread; the Body of our Lord remains whole and entire in each of the parts (CCC 1377).

Q. 92 *Is only the Body of Jesus Christ present under the appearances of bread and only his Blood under the appearances of the wine?*

No, under the appearances of the bread Jesus Christ is present whole and entire, in Body, Blood, Soul, and Divinity; and the same under the appearances of the wine (CCC 1374, 1390).

CHAPTER 26

Preparing Our Hearts For Jesus

"They said to each other, 'Did not our hearts burn within us while he talked to us on the road, while he opened to us the Scriptures?'"

Luke 24:32

When we go up to receive Holy Communion, the priest holds the Host before us and says: "The Body of Christ," to which we respond: "Amen," We are expressing our belief in the Real Presence of Jesus before us under the appearance of bread. We are also remembering that we have been called to unite ourselves with him in this most Holy Sacrament.

All of us are aware of our need for Jesus in our daily lives. Usually we feel this need most when we are suffering or struggling with a difficult problem. Jesus wants us to have confidence in him and not to worry:

Therefore I tell you, do not be anxious about your life, what you shall eat, nor about your body, what you shall put on. For life is more than food, and the body more than clothing. . . . Instead, seek his kingdom, and these things shall be yours as well (Lk 12:22–23, 31).

Receiving Jesus in Holy Communion should be a special occasion for us every time. Like all special occasions, we have to prepare for it. Before you take a big test you put in extra time studying. Or when a special friend comes to visit, you make sure everything is tidy or perhaps even make some sort of gift to give that friend. We must also prepare to receive Jesus in Communion.

Preparing to Receive the Holy Eucharist

Jesus once told a parable about a king who gave a wedding banquet for his son. He invited everyone, rich and poor alike, until his hall was filled. When the king came in to meet his guests, he found one man who had not dressed properly for the wedding feast. When questioned, the man had nothing to say. The king's orders were: "Bind him hand and foot, and cast him into the outer darkness, where there will be weeping and gnashing of teeth" (Mt 22:13).

We will displease Jesus also if we go to Holy Communion without first being properly prepared.

We should always look to the example of Jesus to show us what is necessary. Remember how, at the Last Supper, Jesus washed the feet of his Apostles? This was a sign that we are to receive him with purity and innocence of soul. We are all aware of our unworthiness to receive such a gift, but like the Roman centurion we have confidence that Jesus will make us pleasing in his sight.

So how do we prepare our hearts to receive Jesus? It isn't something we do quickly just before we go to Mass. We should always be ready to meet Jesus. This means that we try to live according to Jesus' teaching. As followers of Jesus, our lives should be filled with prayer and good works. We should be unselfish and always ready to share with anyone in need. And most importantly, we must preserve that special life of grace in us which we first received in Baptism. If we lose that supernatural life through serious (mortal) sin, we should immediately ask God for forgiveness and renew his life in us by going to confession.

The more we know about Jesus, the more we will love him and try to please him and want to be with him. We should receive him in Holy Communion often, with a sincere and humble heart, trusting in his great love and desire to be united with us.

Q. 93 *Is it good and useful to receive Holy Communion frequently?*

It is very good and useful to receive Holy Communion frequently, even every day, provided it is done worthily (CCC 1389).

Q. 94 *How often must a Catholic take part in Mass?*

A Catholic must take part in Mass every Sunday and Holy Day of Obligation (CCC 1389).

Q. 95 *How often must a Catholic receive the Holy Eucharist?*

A Catholic must received Holy Eucharist at least once a year during the Easter season (CCC 1389).

Anima Christi

Soul of Christ, sanctify me.
Body of Christ, save me.
Blood of Christ, inebriate me.
Water from the side of Christ, wash me.
Passion of Christ, strengthen me.
O good Jesus, hear me.
Within thy wounds hide me.
Suffer me not to be separated from thee.
From the malicious enemy defend me.
In the hour of my death call me
And bid me come unto thee,
That with thy saints I may praise thee
For ever and ever. *Amen.*

CHAPTER 27

Come Lord Jesus

"And for their sake I consecrate myself, that they also may be consecrated in truth."

John 17:19

Jesus once asked his disciples, "Who do you say that I am?" Peter answered, "You are the Messiah, the Son of the living God." Jesus rejoiced at this answer because, he said, it was a revelation from God.

Jesus then declared that he would make Peter the Rock, or foundation, upon which he would build his Church. And he said, "I will give you the keys of the kingdom of heaven, and whatever you bind on earth shall be bound in heaven, and whatever you loose on earth shall be loosed in heaven" (Mt 16:19).

The authority to "bind and to loose" includes the authority to administer the Sacraments. In other words, the Church has the power to make rules about these matters. The Church sets the times and circumstances for the Eucharistic sacrifice and for distribution of Holy Communion. She teaches us that there are three necessary conditions for the *worthy* reception of Holy Communion. We must:

1. be in the state of grace;
2. have a right intention;
3. observe the Eucharistic fast.

Let us look at these conditions.

State of Grace

The Church asks us, out of reverence for Christ, to be in the **state of grace**. This means that we may not go to Communion if we have committed a mortal sin and have not yet confessed it. To receive Communion in mortal sin would be another mortal sin, called *sacrilege*, the misuse of something holy. To receive Jesus without being in the state of grace would make us like that man in Jesus' parable who came to the wedding feast without being properly dressed.

Right Intention

To have the right intention, we must be aware of the meaning of the Eucharist: that it is Jesus himself whom we receive under the appearances of bread and wine. This means that we should desire to receive him and do so with humility and modesty, recognizing the fact that God is our Creator and we are his creatures.

How we behave at Mass, especially at Communion time, should reflect all these important attitudes. Looking around and talking to friends expresses disrespect and ignorance and gives a bad example.

We must intend to receive Jesus with faith, understanding, reverence, and a strong desire for the spiritual treasures which are to be had in the Blessed Sacrament.

Eucharistic Fast

The **Eucharistic fast** is a means of preparing to receive Jesus with ample time and consideration. It is a sign of our willingness to free ourselves from our own desires so that we can live as true followers of Christ.

We observe the fast by eating no food and drinking no liquids except water and medicine for one hour before receiving Communion. Those who are advanced in age or suffer from any infirmity, as well as those who take care of them, can receive the Holy Eucharist even if they have taken something during the previous hour.

Thanksgiving

Because the gift we receive in the Eucharist is so great, we should make a sincere thanksgiving afterwards. We may do so in set prayers or in our own words. We may also express thoughts and hopes and fears, our troubles and our joys, our needs and our petitions.

Obligation

After all we have said about how wonderful this Sacrament is, it may be a surprise that the Church has had to make a rule that requires all the faithful to receive the Eucharist at least once a year during the Easter season. The obligation is binding on all who have made their first Communion.

Viaticum

Communion given to one who is dying is called **Viaticum**, a Latin word meaning "provisions for a journey." It is well named. All through life Holy Communion has helped us get ready for a holy death. Viaticum is the final preparation for the journey from life on earth, through death, to life in heaven.

So one departs for that Kingdom about which Saint Paul said: "No eye has seen, nor ear heard, nor the heart of man conceived, what God has prepared for those who love him" (1 Cor 2:9).

We shall thank God then for every worthy and ardent Communion we have received.

Words to Know:
state of grace   Eucharistic fast
Viaticum

Sweetest Jesus, may your most Sacred Body and Blood be the delight and sweetness of my soul, safety and firmness in every temptation, joy and peace in every tribulation, light and strength in every word and work, and final protection in death. *Amen.*

—Saint Thomas Aquinas

Q. 96 *What is necessary for the worthy reception of Holy Communion?*

For the worthy reception of Holy Communion three things are necessary: first, to be in the state of grace; second, to recognize and to consider whom we are about to receive; third, to observe the Eucharistic fast (CCC 1385–87).

Q. 97 *What does it mean to be in the state of grace?*

Being in the state of grace means to be free of all serious sin (CCC 1861).

Q. 98 *How should we receive Holy Communion?*

We should receive Holy Communion reverently and prayerfully. We must be reverent in our behavior and even in our clothing, remembering that we are receiving Jesus Christ as our guest (CCC 1386–87).

Q. 99 *What does the Eucharistic fast require?*

The Eucharistic fast requires one who is to receive the Holy Eucharist to abstain from any food or drink (except for water or medicine) for one hour before Holy Communion (CCC 1387, CIC, Canon 919).

Q. 100 *In danger of death, may one receive Holy Communion even without fasting?*

Yes, in danger of death one may receive Holy Communion without fasting (CCC 1387, CIC, Canon 919, 921).

Q. 101 *What is Viaticum?*

Viaticum is "food for the journey": one's last reception of Holy Communion as he is about to leave this life. It is the Sacrament of passing from death to life (CCC 1524).

CHAPTER 28

His Abiding Presence

"As the Father has loved me, so have I loved you; abide in my love."

John 15:9

We have seen that through transubstantiation Jesus changes bread and wine into his Body and Blood.

The Eucharist is Jesus, Body, Blood, Soul, and Divinity. Jesus is both God and man, and he comes to us in Holy Communion. We receive his divinity as well as his humanity. We can truly say that God becomes our food.

Jesus promised his disciples that he would not leave them orphaned. Indeed, he has instituted a way to stay with us at all times. Jesus is present in the Blessed Sacrament, which is kept in the tabernacles of our churches around the world. A lamp, called the sanctuary lamp, is kept burning there as long as the Blessed Sacrament is in the **tabernacle**.

Here, then, Jesus remains, night and day. He is truly Emmanuel—God with us. He dwells with us full of grace and truth.

We profess our faith in Jesus' presence in the Blessed Sacrament by our behavior in church. Our behavior should include reverent actions: genuflecting, blessing ourselves with holy water, bowing our heads.

We are encouraged to visit the Blessed Sacrament when we have time and a church or chapel is open. The prayer we say there— our conversation with Jesus—is an extra act of love that we offer him freely, and it will bring us special graces.

Eucharistic Worship

The Church has always encouraged devotion to the Blessed Sacrament. There are a number of forms of special Eucharistic worship outside of the Mass, which is, of course, the fountainhead of all the others.

One such form is a Eucharistic procession in which the Blessed Sacrament is carried through the streets with solemnity and reverence, accompanied by singing. Parishes often hold processions on the feast of *Corpus Christi*.

The most common forms of Eucharistic worship outside the Mass, however, are **Exposition** and **Benediction**. The consecrated Host

May the Blessed Sacrament be praised and adored forever.

is put in a **monstrance** and placed on the altar for the faithful to see and adore.

During the Exposition there are prayers and hymns, and usually Jesus is honored with incense. We express our profound adoration before the Real Presence of Christ.

At the end, the priest or deacon lifts the monstrance and blesses the faithful with it in the Sign of the Cross. This is called "Benediction."

Special Devotion

Throughout the ages there have been many saints who have had great devotion to Jesus in the Eucharist. Saint Thomas Aquinas wrote many beautiful hymns for Eucharistic worship.

There is a saint of modern times, Saint Peter Julian Eymard, who founded a religious congregation dedicated to the perpetual adoration of the Real Presence of Christ in the Blessed Sacrament. Priests of this order are called the Blessed Sacrament Fathers. The Blessed Sacrament is always exposed in their religious houses for perpetual adoration.

Words to Know:

tabernacle	Exposition
Benediction	monstrance

Act of Spiritual Communion

My Jesus, I believe that you are in the Blessed Sacrament. I love you above all things, and I long for you in my soul. Since I cannot now receive you sacramentally, come at least spiritually into my heart. I embrace you and unite myself entirely to you; never permit me to be separated from you.

Q. 102 *Is Jesus Christ present in all the consecrated Hosts in the world?*

Yes, Jesus Christ is present in all the consecrated Hosts in the world (CCC 1377).

Q. 103 *Why is the Most Holy Eucharist kept in the churches?*

The Most Holy Eucharist is kept in the churches so that the faithful may adore it, so that they may receive it in Communion, and so that they may recognize in the Holy Eucharist the perpetual assistance and presence of Jesus Christ in the Church (CCC 1378–79).

Q. 104 *Where in the church is the Holy Eucharist kept?*

The Holy Eucharist is kept in a tabernacle, as a worthy place for the presence of the Lord and a place to be recognized by the faithful in Eucharistic devotion (CCC 1379).

PART THREE
The Last Things

CHAPTER 29

Passage into Eternity

"Truly, truly, I say to you, he who hears my word and believes him who sent me, has eternal life; he does not come into judgment, but has passed from death to life."

John 5:24

We are all children of Adam and Eve; we are all made up of body and soul, and condemned by Original Sin to the eventual parting of body and soul that we call death. This parting leaves the body without any life, and it falls back to dust. But the soul does not fall back into nothingness; the soul was made to live forever.

God gave us his very own Son to take the penalty of death upon himself to redeem us from sin. Through Jesus we have the hope of living in heaven with God, although we must still undergo bodily death.

The bishops of the Catholic Church at the Second Vatican Council wrote: "Through Christ and in Christ the riddle of sorrow and death grow meaningful. . . . Apart from his gospel, they overwhelm us."

The mystery of death can only be answered by faith. With faith, we see death as it really is. Jesus said to his Apostles,

"Let not your hearts be troubled; believe in God, believe also in me. In my Father's house are many rooms; if it were not so, would I have told you that I go to prepare a place for you? And when I go and prepare a place for you, I will come again and will take you to

myself, that where I am you may be also. And you know the way where I am going" (Jn 14:1–4).

Every prayer we have ever said, every Sacrament we have received, every good work we have ever done, every grace we have been given, helps to prepare us for the moment of death.

We ought to face death with hopeful joy, for Jesus said to Martha, "I am the resurrection and the life; he who believes in me, though he die, yet shall he live, and whoever lives and believes in me shall never die (Jn 11:25–26).

Particular Judgment

Jesus, who knows our every thought, will judge each of us individually as soon as our souls leave our bodies. This is called the **Particular Judgment**. The truth of his verdict will be made clear to us. With complete clarity we will immediately be aware of three things: 1. the exact balance of good and bad in our life and what we truly are; 2. the perfect justice of our future lot, in heaven or hell; and 3. the presence of the Divine Judge, Jesus.

Saint Paul says: "He will render to every man according to his works: to those who by patience in well-doing seek for glory and honor and immortality, he will give eternal life; but for those who are factious and do not obey the truth, but obey wickedness, there will be wrath and fury" (Rom 2:6–8).

Readiness

Jesus compares us to servants awaiting the return of the master of the house. He said, "Watch therefore—for you do not know when the master of the house will come, in the evening, or at midnight, or at cockcrow, or in the morning" (Mk 13:35).

Jesus recommends a healthy awareness of the reality of death. It should not be a morbid thought; we just have to face facts. If we prepare ourselves for death, we will find joy and peace of mind that death cannot destroy.

We prepare for death by taking advantage of the means our loving Father in heaven has given us. We do our best to live according to his will. We develop a spiritual life of prayer and the Sacraments. We study the truths of our religion in school or in a class at our parish, and afterwards we go on reading on our own and learn more about these truths.

Of course, we are aware that we often fail to keep God's laws, in little things if not in big; and so we must often turn to God's mercy and love. Knowing all this, the Church tells us how we can make up for our sins. We can offer prayers, especially the Rosary; we can do charitable deeds for others; we can do penance and offer sacrifices (for example, give up a dessert or second helping or give up having our own way about a game we are playing with others).

Above all, we should serve God generously, not measuring everything with the minimum required by law. For Jesus said: "With your own measure it will be measured out to you again."

The closer we come to Jesus through prayer and acts of love, the more confidence we will have in his care for us and his mercy. If we live for him, we will learn more and more to see death as the beginning of a new and wonderful life with God.

Words to Know:
Particular Judgment

Prayer for the Dead

Eternal rest grant to them, O Lord, and let perpetual light shine upon them. May they rest in peace.

Q. 105 *What happens to each of us at the end of life?*

At the end of life each of us will die, our body and soul will be separated, and we will face a Particular Judgment (CCC 1005, 1022).

Q. 106 *On what will Jesus Christ judge us?*

Jesus Christ will judge us on the good and evil that we have done in life, including our thoughts, and things we failed to do in response to God's grace (CCC 1021, 1868).

Q. 107 *What happens to each man after the Particular Judgment?*

After the Particular Judgment, those who love God and are perfectly holy go immediately to heaven to be with him. Those who love God but still need purification go to purgatory until they are ready to be with God in heaven. Those who have rejected God, through dying in mortal sin, go to hell (CCC 1022).

CHAPTER 30

Heaven–Purgatory–Hell

"Then the King will say to those at his right hand, 'Come, O blessed of my Father, inherit the kingdom prepared for you from the foundation of the world.'"

Matthew 25:34

Heaven

We cannot know much about heaven, only the little we have been told. Yet every time we look at a crucifix we are reminded that Christ was stripped of everything men hold dear and opened his arms on the Cross to gain for us our everlasting future of unimaginable happiness.

This does not mean that we should not try to think about true happiness, but only that we should always recall that the real thing will be far greater than anything we can think of. We can never make a mistake by exaggerating the happiness of heaven. We can make a great mistake by thinking of it too little. An even greater mistake would be to make heaven sound boring.

Living close to God prepares us for heaven in many ways. Not only does it merit reward, but as the years go by we become more attuned to God and the things of heaven, and that increases our desire to reach heaven and our confidence that we will get there. "O taste and see that the LORD is good!" (Ps 34:8).

The purpose of your life and mine is to see God in heaven someday. But that is not something that is easy to imagine; in fact, we cannot imagine God, since he is a pure spirit and we can only imagine things we have seen. So how can you get an idea of it? You can get an idea

about it by thinking about the beauty and design and order and truth and goodness and power of the world about you. God created every good thing in the world and set it all in order. So the goodness, truth, and beauty of creation give us some idea of God; he is like all these things, but he is infinitely more good, true, and beautiful than all of them. We also have an idea of heaven through everything Jesus said and did.

So now we can ask ourselves this question: What is heaven? And we can say this: Heaven is being with God forever and loving God and living God's own life—which means that we are so united to God that with him we see what he sees, know what he knows, and love how he loves, according to our fullest human capacity. It means that God will make us like himself!

We will not be bored, not for a moment.

Eternal life, therefore, means not only living forever, but living *God's life* forever!

God says: "My people will be filled with my good things."

Purgatory

It's easy to waste time out of thoughtlessness. We should use the minutes, hours, and

126

days to grow in the spiritual life, to come close to God. Our spiritual life begins at Baptism, which removes the punishment for Original Sin but leaves us still with wounds in our nature.

Our life after Baptism, if it is a life of prayer, Sacraments, and good works, will heal our wounds even more; if it is a life of sin and vice, it will deepen them.

There is a book about the spiritual life called *Ascent of Mount Carmel*, by Saint John of the Cross. Growing spiritually is compared to climbing a great mountain. The higher we climb, the more we change. Some people climb all the way to the top and are rewarded with such union with God that they go straight to heaven when they die.

Purgatory can also be compared to the ascent of Mount Carmel. Those who die as God's friends—in the state of grace, free of all sin or attachment to sin, free of all debt to make up for sin—go immediately to heaven when they die. But what about those who die as God's friends, in the state of grace, but with venial sins or unpaid debts for past sins, all forgiven but not yet worked off?

They are not yet ready for heaven. Only what is completely holy can enter heaven. What happens to them?

They go to a place of purification and penance called purgatory where their souls are cleansed and freed of the unpaid debt of sin. Being purified hurts, both here and hereafter; there is no way to be healed and grow that is free from pain. But we can avoid a purgatory in the hereafter by accepting our purgatory here. We can be healed and purified and make up for our sins by doing penance and by humbly accepting the difficulties and sufferings that come to us in life.

In purgatory, there is one thing on everyone's mind: God. The soul there desires God with a greatness that is hard for us to imagine. The souls in purgatory know with absolute certainty that they are saved and are going to heaven. They fear no more danger to their salvation. They are being made ready for union with God, and so they must be cleansed of any obstacles to that perfect union. These obstacles to union are like rust, remains of sin that hinder the soul from enjoying God. Saint Catherine of Genoa tells us that the rust diminishes as the soul becomes healthier under the rays of divine sunlight. So there is great happiness as well as great suffering in purgatory.

The saints in heaven are called the **Church Triumphant**, the souls in purgatory are called the **Church Suffering**, and the faithful on earth are called the **Church Militant**. All together we form the one Church of Christ. We on earth can help the souls in purgatory by praying for them, sacrificing for them, and offering Masses for them.

Hell

Jesus told us that just as those who do the will of the Father will receive the reward of eternal happiness, those who reject the Father and refuse to do the will of God will be condemned to eternal punishment. "Depart from me, you cursed, into the eternal fire prepared for the devil and his angels" (Mt 25:41). The condemned are those who die without repenting of their mortal sins.

Many people like to think that hell does not exist. They say that God would never send anyone to a place of everlasting torment since he loves us so much. It is true that God does not want people to go there. But he made us with a free will so that we could freely choose to love God. Any persons in hell have freely chosen to love only themselves and have chosen not to love God; they are, of their own choosing, utterly alone.

The loss of God is the greatest pain in hell. We were made for God, but since the souls in hell have totally rejected him there is nothing left for which they can hope. And what makes their suffering in hell even greater is that each one there will realize that he alone is the cause of his own damnation.

God offers everyone the grace to repent and turn to him. We should always remember to pray for those who are near death so that they will seek the mercy that God extends to them.

Words to Know:
Church Triumphant   Church Suffering
Church Militant

"For what does it profit a man, to gain the whole world and forfeit his life? For what can a man give in return for his life? For whoever is ashamed of me and of my words in this adulterous and sinful generation, of him will the Son of man also be ashamed, when he comes in the glory of his Father with the holy angels" (Mark 8:36–38).

Q. 108 *What is eternal life?*

Eternal life is the reward of living forever with God in the happiness of heaven. The souls of those who die in grace and God's friendship enter heaven after death, either immediately or after purification (CCC 1022).

Q. 109 *What is heaven?*

Heaven is our eternal enjoyment of God, who is our happiness, with the angels and the blessed (CCC 1023–24).

Q. 110 *What is purgatory?*

Purgatory is the temporary state of purifying suffering after death for those who die in God's friendship, but who do not yet have the holiness needed to be with God in heaven (CCC 1030–31).

Q. 111 *What is hell?*

Hell is the eternal suffering of separation from God (CCC 1033–35).

Q. 112 *Is it certain that heaven and hell exist?*

Yes, it is certain that heaven and hell exist. God has revealed this, frequently promising eternal life and happiness with him to the good, and threatening the wicked with damnation and eternal fire (CCC 1024, 1034).

Q. 113 *How long will heaven and hell last?*

Heaven and hell will last forever (CCC 1029, 1035).

CHAPTER 31

He Shall Come Again

"And when I go and prepare a place for you, I will come again and will take you to myself, that where I am you may be also."

John 14:3

Saint Luke records in the Acts of the Apostles that at Jesus' Ascension into heaven, two angels stood by the disciples and said to them, "Men of Galilee, why do you stand looking into heaven? This Jesus, who was taken up from you into heaven, will come in the same way as you saw him go into heaven" (Acts 1:11).

One day, when we least expect it, Jesus will appear in the heavens in great splendor and majesty, and all the armies of heaven with him. At this **Second Coming**, the trumpets will sound, the dead will rise, and the whole human race will be assembled before the judgment seat of Christ; the books will be opened and the judgment will begin. Every man's deeds, even the most secret, will be made known. Everyone will see and appreciate the holiness of the just, whether they hardly ever sinned or were great sinners and overcame their sins. Everyone will see and appreciate the justice of God in banishing the unrepentant from his sight, into hell forever.

The just, who served God with body and soul, in good times and bad, in good health and sickness, in joy and in sorrow, in pleasure and pain, will now receive a wonderful, glorious reward. They have tried hard to do something

beautiful for God; now God will do something beautiful for them. It is true that they already see God, and this is called the Beatific Vision because it is a vision, a knowledge, which "beatifies" us, or makes us *completely* happy. Nevertheless, the souls in heaven are not yet all that God made them to be. Man was not made to be a disembodied spirit; man is a creature composed of body and soul. The body and soul will be brought together again at the Second Coming. It is the whole man who will enjoy heaven or suffer in hell. There will no longer be any need for purgatory.

One of the reasons for the judgment at the end of the world, called the **General Judgment**, is to make clear to everyone the wisdom, knowledge, graciousness, mercy, patience, loving kindness, and justice of the Lord of history in his dealings with all men. All shall be satisfied that it was well done. Then the just, who so often suffered at the hands of the unjust, will be honored, and the unjust who refused to ask God's forgiveness will be covered with shame and disgrace.

Above all, Jesus Christ the Savior, who suffered such humiliations, will be fully vindicated, exalted, glorified, and honored. His splendor will be so great that he will light up the whole City of God. In the City of God, the new Jerusalem, the heavenly city, the whole universe will be renewed and set free from anything unfitting or harmful. Then those who have loved God and lived in his light will be united with him in heaven. And the just will have tremendous powers of mind and body to enjoy it all.

This is the goal toward which we are all striving. Remember how Saint Paul compared the life of a Christian to an athlete's? Let us work toward our goal so that we can say with him:

I have fought the good fight, I have finished the race, I have kept the faith. From now on there is laid up for me the crown of righteousness, which the Lord, the righteous judge, will award to me on that Day, and not only to me but also to all who have loved his appearing (2 Tim 4:7–8).

Words to Know:
Second Coming   General Judgment

**We proclaim your Death, O Lord,
and profess your Resurrection
until you come again.**

Q. 114 *Will Jesus Christ visibly return to earth?*

Yes, Jesus Christ will visibly return to this earth at the end of the world to judge the living and the dead, at the General Judgment (CCC 680–82).

Q. 115 *What awaits us at the end of the world?*

The resurrection of the body and the General Judgment await us at the end of the world (CCC 1016, 1038).

Q. 116 *What does "resurrection of the body" mean?*

The "resurrection of the body" means that our bodies will be transformed by the power of God and reunited with our souls, so that we will share in the eternal reward or punishment we have merited (CCC 997–99, 1005).

Christmas Season Supplement

Angels We Have Heard on High

"Glory to God in the highest, and on earth peace among men with whom he is pleased!"

Luke 2:14

Legend has it that Saint Francis of Assisi put together the first manger scene for Christmas with figures to inspire devotion—and that was about eight hundred years ago. The story of the birth of the Son of God has an endless appeal. For, considering who Jesus is, he chose for himself the humblest possible birth. He had every right to be born in a palace; he was born in a stable. He had every right to many servants; at most he had an ox and a donkey.

The Son of God did not come into the world with power and glory. He did not come to establish an earthly kingdom. He came to redeem the human race from sin. His birth was the first step toward that end.

The Gospel tells us that the birth of Jesus came in "the fullness of time," that is, at the time God had chosen and prepared. He chose a virgin, Mary of Nazareth, to be the Mother of his Son, and let her remain a virgin before and after his birth. Isaiah the prophet had written: "Therefore the Lord himself will give you a sign. Behold, a virgin shall conceive and bear a son, and shall call his name Immanuel" (Is 7:14).

God chose Mary from among all Jewish women to be the Mother of his Son. He also protected her from Original Sin, which has been passed on to every other descendant of Adam, except Jesus himself. Mary possessed God's grace from the first moment of her existence. It would not have been fitting for God

the Son to receive his humanity from a sinful woman. Mary's conception without Original Sin is called the Immaculate Conception. "Immaculate" means "pure" or "spotless."

Mary's soul, then, was pure and spotless. She was "full of grace" because God had saved her from Original Sin and all actual sin. She never sinned—not once, not even in the smallest way. She loved God so much. Mary was first in importance, after Jesus, among all the people who played a major role in God's plan of redemption. But she was not an earthly princess. She lived with her parents in a small town of Nazareth. She was betrothed to a man named Joseph, a carpenter.

Mary was still a young girl, betrothed to Saint Joseph, when God sent an angel to her on a very special mission. She must have been startled. The archangel Gabriel told her not to be afraid. He told her that she had found favor with God and had been chosen to be the Mother of the Savior. He told her that she would conceive the Child by the power of the Holy Spirit; thus, she would always remain a virgin. Furthermore, the Child would be called "Son of God."

Mary's answer was: "Behold, I am the handmaid of the Lord; let it be to me according to your word" (Lk 1:38).

Then the angel left her, and God worked the miracle in which his only Son was conceived in her womb without an earthly father. When it became clear that Mary was going to bear a child, the same angel, Gabriel, told Joseph, Mary's betrothed, that Mary was with child by the Holy Spirit. This Child, he told Joseph, was to be named Jesus, because he would save his people from their sins. The angel told Joseph not to be concerned.

Joseph was relieved to hear the angel's message. He had been anxious about his life with Mary. He had not understood about Mary

conceiving a child without a human father, and he had wondered about God's plan for him as Mary's husband. Now Joseph and Mary together prepared for the Child's birth.

Not long before the Child was due, the Roman emperor decreed that there should be a census of the whole empire. Joseph had to take Mary with him to Bethlehem, the town of his ancestors, to register there for the census.

This involved a trip of about ninety miles, which must have been uncomfortable for Mary in her condition. Then, after the dusty, crowded roads, they found the houses and hotels in Bethlehem already filled. After asking everywhere, Joseph led his beloved wife to a stable, a cave in a hillside where she would be out of the cold night air and have privacy; and there, in that stable, the Son of God was born. There he gave his first cry and was laid down to sleep on some straw in a manger. He was wrapped in strips of cloth called swaddling clothes.

In the fields on some nearby hills, unusual things were happening. Angels came to some shepherds and told them to go to the stable to see the newborn Savior of the world. When the angels disappeared, the shepherds did what they had been told and found the Child. They were the first to see him. These shepherds weren't very powerful or important people, but they had what is always needed to find Jesus: humility. When they saw him, Luke tells us, they "understood" what they had been told about the Child.

Who Is Jesus?

When Jesus cried, or felt chilled, or became hungry, it was God crying, or feeling chilled, or becoming hungry. He is the Son of God made man—that is, true God and true man. Before becoming man, he had eternal, infinite life with God the Father and God the Holy Spirit in the Blessed Trinity. This life was never interrupted; even after becoming man he remains God.

Jesus is one Person, God the Son, with two natures, divine and human. As God, he can do everything God can do (know everything, create out of nothing, raise the dead, be everywhere, live eternally, love without limit), and as man he can do everything man can do—which is surely much less than what God can do.

The act by which the Son of God became man is called the Incarnation—which means, literally, taking on flesh. This happened when he was conceived in the womb of the Blessed Virgin Mary, and it was revealed for all the world to see when he was born.

That's how much God loved us—enough to become one of us.

Q. 117 *How did God prepare Mary to be the Mother of his Son?*

God prepared Mary to be the Mother of his Son by preserving her from Original Sin, which means that she was filled with grace from the moment of her conception. This is called the Immaculate Conception (CCC 491).

Q. 118 *What is the mystery of God made man called?*

The mystery of God made man is called the Incarnation (CCC 470).

Q. 119 *Did the Son of God cease to be God when he became man?*

No, the Son of God did not cease to be God when he became man. God is eternal (CCC 470).

Q. 120 *Is Jesus true God and true man?*

Yes, Jesus is true God and true man. He has two natures: human and divine (CCC 464).

Q. 121 *Is Jesus two persons?*

No, Jesus is one Divine Person, the Second Person of the Blessed Trinity (CCC 466).

Fruit Upon the Bough: The Mission

"... for my eyes have seen your salvation which you have prepared in the presence of all peoples, a light for revelation to the Gentiles, and for glory to your people Israel."

Luke 2:30–32

In his great mercy God gave to us his own Son to restore us to his friendship. Christ came into the world as an infant, bore witness to the will of the Father, taught us the complete truth about God, and was himself the perfect model of all we should be.

We call this Christ's mission. Even in Jesus' infancy, God began to reveal this mission to the world. We have seen how the shepherds were invited to come and see the

newborn Savior. Not long afterward, other things happened that showed that God was letting people know about Jesus' mission.

When Jesus was eight days old, Saint Luke tells us he was circumcised in accordance with Jewish law; when he was forty days old, he was presented to the Lord in the temple in Jerusalem. His parents offered in sacrifice two young pigeons, as the law directed.

Then a most unusual thing happened. A very devout old man named Simeon was led by the Holy Spirit to the Child in the temple and took him into his arms. Through the Holy Spirit he recognized the Messiah. With great joy Simeon blessed God, saying that now he could die in peace because he had seen the Savior both of the Jews and Gentiles. Mary and Joseph marveled at what was being said.

Then the shadow of the Cross fell across the group—the Cross which was still far in the future. Simeon turned to Mary and said: "Behold, this child is set for the fall and rising of many in Israel, and for a sign that is spoken against (and a sword will pierce through your own soul also), that thoughts out of many hearts may be revealed" (Lk 2:34–35).

Simeon saw a full picture: power, glory, and suffering. The Child was a sign that would be opposed—and Mary, His mother and the Mother of the Church, would have a unique share in his sufferings. God was filling in the picture of his plan of redemption.

Shortly afterward, three kings or wise men from the East came to see the Child and give him gifts. God had told them to follow a bright star to find the newborn King of the Jews. Their visit was added testimony to the greatness of the newborn Savior; it was also testimony to the all-out fury which would oppose him.

King Herod, a vicious man insanely jealous of his power, heard from the wise men that a new King had been born, and all his darkest passions were aroused. Intending to kill the Child, he instructed the wise men to report back to him after they had found the Child. But the wise men were warned against Herod in a dream, and they went home by another route after their visit.

When Herod learned of this, his rage and suspicion knew no bounds. He sent his soldiers to Bethlehem and the surrounding area with orders to kill all the boys there who were two years old and younger, being certain that the newborn King would perish in the holocaust.

However, the Holy Family escaped the clutches of this bloodthirsty tyrant. Joseph had been warned in a dream of the coming danger. An angel commanded him to take mother and child and seek safety in Egypt and to stay there until he was told it was safe to come home.

Joseph obeyed immediately—that very night—and so they escaped. The children who died were Christ's first martyrs. We call them the Holy Innocents.

Not everybody is called to give his life for Christ—though many have. But it is sometimes as difficult to live for Christ as it is to die for him. It may even be harder. Take the case of a person with a serious illness who nevertheless has to bear heavy responsibilities. Think of Saint John Paul II, who had to

resume the burdensome task of the papacy after being so badly wounded. That must be harder than dying.

Another Stage

When Jesus was twelve years old, Luke tells us, he went to Jerusalem with his parents for the feast of the Passover. Unknown to them, he stayed behind when they set out on their return. At the end of the day they discovered he wasn't with them and returned immediately to Jerusalem to look for him. The third day they found him in the temple, deeply involved in conversation with the teachers of the law, listening to them and asking them questions. Everyone who heard him was amazed at his wisdom.

Mary asked him why he had done this. He answered, "Didn't you know that I must be about my Father's business?" His parents did not understand. Afterwards he returned with them to Nazareth and lived in obedience, and Mary thought over all these things while he "increased in wisdom and in stature, and in favor with God and man" (Lk 2:52).

The unfolding of Christ's mission was often mysterious, even to his parents. In the temple he had said, in effect, that he had reached adulthood, like turning eighteen or twenty-one in our society. According to Jewish law he was a man; and now that Jesus was an adult, the Father wanted his Son's witness in the temple. He wanted his Son's wisdom to be known. But only this hint was given when Jesus was young; we hear no more until he is thirty years old and begins his public life. "Let your light shine before men," he was to say; and when he was twelve years old, he had begun to do so.

Until he entered upon his public life, Jesus lived quietly in poverty and humility, obedient in all things to the authority of his parents. His whole life is a mystery of redemption.

Q. 122 *In what ways is Jesus' whole life a mystery of redemption?*
Jesus' whole life is a mystery of redemption by God's act of becoming man in the Incarnation which brought us a share in his life, by Jesus' obedience which atoned for our disobedience, by Jesus' miracles and healings through which he bore our infirmities, and by his death and Resurrection which justifies man (CCC 517).

Liturgical Colors and Vestments

ALB: a full-length white tunic worn by the priest when offering Mass.

AMICE: an oblong piece of white cloth worn by the priest under the alb covering his shoulders.

CHALICE: the cup-shaped vessel used at Mass to contain the Precious Blood of Christ.

CHASUBLE: the outer garment worn by the priest celebrating Mass.

CIBORIUM: a vessel with a lid used to hold the consecrated Hosts which we receive in Holy Communion.

CINCTURE: a cord tied around the waist of the alb.

COPE: a large semi-circular cloak worn by the priest at Benediction and in processions.

CORPORAL: a square white linen cloth on which the paten and chalice are placed during Mass.

CRUETS: small bottles or vessels that contain the water and wine used during Mass.

DALMATIC: the outer garment worn by a deacon at Mass or other liturgical celebrations.

FINGER TOWEL: a cloth used by the priest to dry his hands during the Mass.

HUMERAL VEIL: a long, oblong piece of cloth worn like a shawl over the priest's shoulders during Benediction when the priest holds the monstrance.

LAVABO DISH or FINGER BOWL: a shallow dish for the water used when the priest washes his hands at Mass.

PALL: a stiff, square card covered with white linen used to cover the chalice at Mass.

PATEN: a plate of precious material on which the Body of Christ is placed during Mass.

PURIFICATOR: a small white linen towel used by the priest to purify the chalice and paten after Communion.

alb

amice

chalice

chasuble

ciborium

cincture

cope

corporal

STOLE: a long, narrow strip of cloth worn around the priest's neck during Mass; it is the same color as the chasuble.

VESTMENTS: special garments worn by the clergy at all liturgical celebrations. At Mass these include the amice, alb, cincture, stole, and chasuble. For Benediction the cope and humeral veil are used.

LITURGICAL COLORS

The different colors used throughout the liturgical year for vestments and decorations in the Church symbolize various truths and sentiments of the Faith.

WHITE: symbolizes purity, joy, innocence, holiness, and glory; it is used during the Christmas and Easter seasons, for feasts and commemorations of Christ (other than the Passion) and for feasts and memorials of Mary, the angels, and saints who were not martyrs, and it may be used for Masses of the dead.

RED: symbolizes fire and blood; used for celebrations of the Passion, Palm Sunday, Good Friday, for Pentecost, for feasts of the Apostles and evangelists, and for feasts of martyrs.

GREEN: symbolizes life and hope; used for days which are not feasts during Ordinary Time (the time after Epiphany up to Ash Wednesday and after Pentecost up to Advent).

VIOLET: symbolizes penitence and sorrow; used during the penitential seasons of Advent and Lent. It may also be used for Masses of the dead.

ROSE: is an indication of a more joyful celebration, and is used on Gaudete Sunday during Advent and Laetare Sunday during Lent.

BLACK: symbolizes mourning; it may be used in Masses for the dead and on All Souls' Day.

cruets   dalmatic

finger towel   humeral veil

pall   paten

purificator   stole

Words to Know

ABSTINENCE: a form of penance such as refraining from eating meat.

ADORATION: giving praise and honor.

ADVENT: the liturgical season starting four Sundays before Christmas, during which we prepare for the birth of Jesus.

APOSTASY: the rejection by a baptized person of the Christian Faith.

AVARICE: excessive desire for wealth; greed.

BEATITUDE: the promise of true happiness made by Jesus to those who follow him faithfully.

BENEDICTION: When the priest blesses the people with Jesus in the Blessed Sacrament.

BLASPHEMY: the sin of speaking about or to God in a scornful or irreverent way.

CHASTITY: the virtue of ordering sexual pleasures according to the Sixth and Ninth Commandments.

CHURCH MILITANT: the members of the Church on earth.

CHURCH SUFFERING: the souls in purgatory.

CHURCH TRIUMPHANT: the saints in heaven.

CONSCIENCE: our ability to know and judge what is right or wrong.

COVENANT: a solemn agreement.

CULPABLE IGNORANCE: not knowing something that one ought to know.

CURSING: the sin of expressing hope that evil or harm will happen to someone or something.

DECALOGUE: the Ten Commandments given to Moses by God.

DETRACTION: the sin of telling something without sufficient reason about another person that is true but harmful to that person's reputation.

DIOCESE: the part of the Church over which a bishop has authority.

DIVINE OFFICE: the prayer of the Church using Psalms, hymns, and readings. It is called the Liturgy of the Hours because parts of it may be prayed at different times of the day.

DOXOLOGY: A prayer of adoration and praise, said especially in honor of the Blessed Trinity. The prayer said by the priest after the Consecration: "Through him, with him, in him. . ." is an example of a doxology.

ENVY: the sin of being resentful or saddened by another's success.

EUCHARIST: the real Body and Blood of Jesus under the appearances of bread and wine.

EUCHARISTIC FAST: abstinence from food and drink one hour before receiving Holy Communion. Water and medicine do not break the Eucharistic fast. The aged, the sick, and those who care for them may receive the Eucharist even if they have taken something during the previous hour.

EXPOSITION: the ceremony in which the Sacred Host is placed in a monstrance on or above the altar for adoration.

FALSE WITNESS: the giving of untrue testimony about another; lying about someone.

FASTING: doing penance by eating less food than usual.

FLATTERY: false praise.

FRAUD: the sin of deceiving another in order to deprive him of something he rightfully owns.

GENERAL JUDGMENT: the universal judgment of the entire human race at the end of the world.

GOSSIP: the sin of idle or malicious talk about others.

HERESY: the willful denial of a truth of Faith.

HEROIC VIRTUE: the performance of extraordinarily virtuous actions.

HOLY DAYS OF OBLIGATION: certain days, besides Sundays, when Catholics are required to take part in Holy Mass.

HONOR: to respect and reverence someone or something.

HOSANNA: a Hebrew word meaning "save us." It is a special exclamation of joy at the salvation God has promised us.

IDOLATRY: the sin of worshipping something other than God.

IMMACULATE CONCEPTION: Mary's conception free of the stain of Original Sin. Through the grace of God, Mary was free from Original Sin from the moment of her conception.

IMPIETY: the sin of lacking reverence or proper respect for God.

IMPURITY: sexual pleasure in thought or action that is against the Sixth or Ninth Commandments.

INTERCESSOR: someone who pleads or prays for another.

LAST SUPPER: the last meal Jesus had with his Apostles, at which he gave us the Eucharist, the Mass, and the priesthood.

LENT: the liturgical season of penance in preparation for Easter.

LITURGY: the public ceremonies of the Church used for worship.

LITURGY OF THE HOURS: see Divine Office.

MAKE SATISFACTION FOR: making up for some wrong-doing.

MEMORIAL: the recalling or remembrance of a past event.

MONSTRANCE: a special vessel used to hold and display the Sacred Host for adoration.

MURDER: the sin of killing someone wrongfully.

MYSTERY: a divinely revealed truth which we can never fully understand.

OATH: a declaration calling on God as a witness to the truth of what is being said.

OBLATION: the offering of something in an act of worship.

PARTICULAR JUDGMENT: the individual judgment by Christ of each human being at the moment after death.

PASSOVER: the Jewish feast commemorating the deliverance of the Israelites from Egypt.

PATRON SAINT: a special saint chosen to intercede for a particular person or group.

PENANCE: something done to make up for sin.

PRAYER: the raising of the mind and heart to God; talking with God.

PRECEPT: a particular rule or command.

RASH JUDGMENT: the sin of judging another's behavior as wrong without enough evidence.

REVERENCE: honor and respect.

SABBATH: the day of rest and worship; it is celebrated on Saturday by the Jews and on Sunday by Christians.

SACRAMENT: a sign given by Jesus that gives us grace.

SACRIFICE: the offering up of something to God.

SAINTS: holy people, particularly those whom the Church has declared to be in heaven.

SANCTITY: holiness.

SCANDAL: the sin of giving bad example which leads another into sin.

SECOND COMING: the return of Jesus at the end of the world as he promised at his Ascension.

SELF-DENIAL: the act of giving up something we desire for a higher motive.

SLANDER: the sin of saying something false about another which harms his good name.

STATE OF GRACE: being free of mortal sin and possessing God's grace.

STEALING: the sin of taking the property of another; this is a sin against the Seventh Commandment.

SUICIDE: the act of killing oneself; this is a sin against the Fifth Commandment. (However, if someone commits suicide without full knowledge and consent, his responsibility before God is lessened, even though the act is still wrong.)

SUPERSTITION: belief that creatures have supernatural powers.

TABERNACLE: a container in our churches in which the Blessed Sacrament is reserved.

TEN COMMANDMENTS: the laws given to us by God.

TRANSUBSTANTIATION: the complete change of substance of the bread and wine into the Body and Blood of Christ.

USURY: the sin of taking excessive interest for a loan of money.

VIATICUM: Holy Communion given to someone in danger of death.

VICAR OF CHRIST: the Pope, who takes the place of Jesus on earth.

VICTIM: the thing offered to God in a sacrifice.

VOLUNTARY DOUBT: the sin of willfully doubting some religious truth when there is enough reason to believe it.

VOW: a solemn promise made to God of something good and pleasing to him.

WORSHIP: giving honor, praise, and sacrifice to God.

Prayers

THE SIGN OF THE CROSS

In the name of the Father, and of the Son, and of the Holy Spirit. *Amen.*

OUR FATHER

Our Father who art in heaven, hallowed be thy name. Thy kingdom come. Thy will be done on earth, as it is in heaven. Give us this day our daily bread, and forgive us our trespasses, as we forgive those who trespass against us, and lead us not into temptation, but deliver us from evil. *Amen.*

HAIL MARY

Hail Mary, full of grace, the Lord is with thee. Blessed art thou among women, and blessed is the fruit of thy womb, Jesus.

Holy Mary, Mother of God, pray for us sinners now and at the hour of our death. *Amen.*

GLORY BE

Glory be to the Father, and to the Son, and to the Holy Spirit. As it was in the beginning, is now, and ever shall be, world without end. *Amen.*

MORNING OFFERING

O Jesus, through the Immaculate Heart of Mary, I offer thee my prayers, works, joys, and sufferings of this day in union with the Holy Sacrifice of the Mass throughout the world.

I offer them for all the intentions of thy Sacred Heart: the salvation of souls, reparation for sin, the reunion of all Christians.

I offer them for the intentions of our Bishops and of all Apostles of Prayer, and in particular for those recommended by our Holy Father this month. *Amen.*

THE APOSTLES' CREED

I believe in God,
the Father almighty,
Creator of heaven and earth,
and in Jesus Christ,
his only Son, our Lord,
who was conceived by the Holy Spirit,
born of the Virgin Mary,
suffered under Pontius Pilate,
was crucified, died, and was buried;
he descended into hell;
on the third day he rose again
from the dead;
he ascended into heaven,
and is seated at the right
hand of God the Father almighty;
from there he will come to judge
the living and the dead.
I believe in the Holy Spirit,
the holy catholic Church,
the communion of saints,
the forgiveness of sins,
the resurrection of the body,
and life everlasting. *Amen.*

ACT OF FAITH

O my God, I firmly believe that thou art one God in three Divine Persons: Father, Son, and Holy Spirit. I believe that thy Divine Son became man and died for our sins, and that he will come to judge the living and the dead. I believe these and all the truths that the Holy Catholic Church teaches, because thou hast revealed them, who can neither deceive nor be deceived. *Amen.*

ACT OF HOPE

O my God, relying on thy infinite goodness and promises, I hope to obtain pardon of my sins, the help of thy grace, and life everlasting, through the merits of Jesus Christ, my Lord and Redeemer. *Amen.*

ACT OF LOVE

O my God, I love thee above all things, with my whole heart and soul, because thou art all good and worthy of all my love. I love my neighbor as myself for the love of thee. I forgive all who have injured me and ask pardon of all whom I have injured. *Amen.*

ACT OF CONTRITION

O my God, I am heartily sorry for having offended thee. I detest all my sins because of thy just punishments, but most of all because they offend thee, my God, who art all good and deserving of all my love. I firmly resolve, with the help of thy grace, to confess my sins, to do penance, and to amend my life. *Amen.*

THE ANGELUS

V. The angel of the Lord declared unto Mary.
R. And she conceived of the Holy Spirit.

Hail Mary. . . .

V. Behold the handmaid of the Lord.
R. Be it done to me according to thy word.

Hail Mary. . . .

V. And the Word was made flesh.
R. And dwelt among us.

Hail Mary. . . .

V. Pray for us, O holy Mother of God.
R. That we may be made worthy of the promises of Christ.

Let us pray. Pour forth, we beseech thee, O Lord, thy grace into our hearts, that we, to whom the Incarnation of Christ thy Son was made known by the message of an angel, may by his Passion and Cross be brought to the glory of his Resurrection. Through the same Christ our Lord. *Amen.*

MYSTERIES OF THE ROSARY

The Joyful Mysteries

1. The Annunciation.
2. The Visitation.
3. The Nativity.
4. The Presentation.
5. The Finding in the Temple.

The Sorrowful Mysteries

1. The Agony in the Garden.
2. The Scourging at the Pillar.
3. The Crowning with Thorns.
4. The Carrying of the Cross.
5. The Crucifixion.

The Glorious Mysteries

1. The Resurrection.
2. The Ascension.
3. The Descent of the Holy Spirit.
4. The Assumption.
5. The Coronation.

Optional: The Luminous Mysteries

1. The Baptism of Christ in the Jordan.
2. The Wedding Feast of Cana.
3. The Proclamation of the Kingdom of God.
4. The Transfiguration of Our Lord.
5. The Institution of the Holy Eucharist.

LITANY OF LORETO

Lord, have mercy on us.
Christ, have mercy on us.
Lord, have mercy on us.
Christ, hear us.
Christ, graciously hear us.
God the Father of heaven,
have mercy on us.
God the Son, Redeemer of the world,
have mercy on us.
God the Holy Spirit,
have mercy on us.
Holy Trinity, One God,
have mercy on us.

Holy Mary, *pray for us.**
Holy Mother of God,
Holy Virgin of virgins,
Mother of Christ,
Mother of divine grace,
Mother most pure,
Mother most chaste,
Mother inviolate,
Mother undefiled,
Mother most amiable,
Mother most admirable,
Mother of good counsel,
Mother of the Church,
Mother of our Creator,
Mother of our Savior,
Virgin most prudent,
Virgin most venerable,
Virgin most renowned,
Virgin most powerful,
Virgin most merciful,
Virgin most faithful,
Mirror of justice,
Seat of wisdom,
Cause of our joy,
Spiritual vessel,
Vessel of honor,
Singular vessel of devotion,

Pray for us is repeated after each invocation.

Mystical rose,
Tower of David,
Tower of ivory,
House of gold,
Ark of the covenant,
Gate of heaven,
Morning star,
Health of the sick,
Refuge of sinners,
Comforter of the afflicted,
Help of Christians,
Queen of Angels,
Queen of Patriarchs,
Queen of Prophets,
Queen of Apostles,
Queen of Martyrs,
Queen of Confessors,
Queen of Virgins,
Queen of all Saints,
Queen conceived without Original Sin,
Queen assumed into heaven,
Queen of the most holy Rosary,
Queen of peace,

Lamb of God, who take away the sins of the world, *spare us, O Lord.*
Lamb of God, who take away the sins of the world, *graciously hear us, O Lord.*
Lamb of God, who take away the sins of the world, *have mercy on us.*

Pray for us, O holy Mother of God.
That we may be made worthy of the promises of Christ.

Let us pray: Grant, we beseech Thee, O Lord God, unto us Thy servants, that we may rejoice in continual health of mind and body; and, by the glorious intercession of blessed Mary ever virgin, may be delivered from present sadness, and enter into the joy of Thine eternal gladness. Through Christ our Lord. *Amen.*

THE STATIONS OF THE CROSS

1. Jesus is condemned to death.
2. Jesus carries his Cross.
3. Jesus falls the first time.
4. Jesus meets his Mother.
5. Jesus is helped by Simon of Cyrene.
6. Veronica wipes the face of Jesus.
7. Jesus falls a second time.
8. Jesus speaks to the women.
9. Jesus falls a third time.
10. Jesus is stripped of his clothes.
11. Jesus is nailed to the Cross.
12. Jesus dies on the Cross.
13. Jesus is taken down from the Cross.
14. Jesus is placed in the tomb.

PRAYER FOR THE POPE

Father of Providence, look with love on *N.* our Pope, your appointed successor to Saint Peter on whom you built your Church. May he be the visible center and foundation of our unity in faith and love. Grant this through our Lord Jesus Christ, your Son, who lives and reigns with you and the Holy Spirit, one God, for ever and ever. *Amen.*

PRAYER FOR A BISHOP

Lord our God, you have chosen your servant *N.* to be a shepherd of your flock in the tradition of the Apostles. Give him a spirit of courage and right judgment, a spirit of knowledge and love. By governing with fidelity those entrusted to his care may he build your Church as a sign of salvation for the world. We ask this through our Lord Jesus Christ, your Son, who lives and reigns with you and the Holy Spirit, one God, for ever and ever. *Amen.*

PRAYER FOR VOCATIONS
by SAINT JOHN PAUL II

O Jesus, our Good Shepherd, bless all our parishes with numerous priests, deacons, men and women in religious life, consecrated laity and missionaries, according to the needs of the entire world, which you love and wish to save.

We especially entrust our community to you; grant us the spirit of the first Christians, so that we may be a cenacle of prayer, in loving acceptance of the Holy Spirit and his gifts.

Assist our pastors and all who live a consecrated life. Guide the steps of those who have responded generously to your call and are preparing to receive holy orders or to profess the evangelical counsels.

Look with love on so many well-disposed young people and call them to follow you. Help them to understand that in you alone can they attain to complete fulfillment.

To this end we call on the powerful intercession of Mary, Mother and Model of all vocations. We beseech you to sustain our faith with the certainty that the Father will grant what you have commanded us to ask. *Amen.*

PRAYER FOR
UNITY OF THE CHURCH

Almighty and merciful God, you willed that the different nations should become one people through your Son. Grant in your kindness that those who glory in being known as Christians may put aside their differences and become one in truth and charity, and that all men, enlightened by the true faith, may be united in fraternal communion in the one Church. Through Christ our Lord. *Amen.*

ANIMA CHRISTI

Soul of Christ, sanctify me.
Body of Christ, save me.
Blood of Christ, inebriate me.
Water from the side of Christ, wash me.
Passion of Christ, strengthen me.
O good Jesus, hear me;
Within thy wounds hide me;
Suffer me not to be separated from thee;
From the malignant enemy defend me;
In the hour of my death call me,
And bid me come to Thee,
That with Thy Saints I may praise Thee
for ever and ever. *Amen.*

MEMORARE

Remember, O most gracious Virgin Mary, that never was it known that anyone who fled to thy protection, implored thy help, or sought thy intercession, was left unaided. Inspired with this confidence, I fly unto thee, O Virgin of Virgins, my Mother: to thee do I come, before thee I stand, sinful and sorrowful. O Mother of the Word Incarnate, despise not my petitions, but in thy mercy hear and answer me. *Amen.*

PRAYER TO SAINT MICHAEL

Saint Michael, the Archangel, defend us in battle. Be our protection against the wickedness and snares of the devil. May God rebuke him, we humbly pray, and do thou, O prince of the heavenly hosts, by the power of God, thrust into hell Satan and the other evil spirits who prowl about the world seeking the ruin of souls. *Amen.*

EXAMINATION OF CONSCIENCE

How have I acted toward God? Do I think of God and speak to Him by praying to Him each day?

Do I speak of God with reverence?

Do I go to Mass on Sunday?

Do I do all I can to make Sunday a day of rest and joy for my family?

Do I participate in Mass, or do I tease or distract others by laughing, talking, or playing?

Do I pay attention to my parents, priests, and teachers when they talk to me about God?

How have I acted toward others?

Do I obey my parents and teachers quickly and cheerfully, or must I be reminded many times?

Do I tell my parents or those in authority over me that I am sorry and ask them to forgive me when I have not minded them?

Do I obey the rules of my home and school?

Do I help my brothers, sisters, and classmates when they need my help?

Am I kind to everyone?

Did I hit, kick, or in any way hurt others on purpose?

Am I willing to play with everyone?

Did I make fun or say mean things to anyone?

Do I do all my classwork and my chores at home well?

Do I take care of my health by eating the right food, etc.?

Do I think or do bad things or say bad words?

Do I tell the truth?

Do I say things about other people that are not true?

Did I cheat in class or in a game?

Did I steal or keep things that are not mine?

Am I willing to share my things with others?

Do I return things that I have borrowed?

THE PRAYER OF FATIMA

O my Jesus, forgive us our sins, save us from the fires of hell, and lead all souls into heaven, especially those in most need of thy mercy. *Amen.*

SPIRITUAL COMMUNION

My Jesus, as I cannot receive thee now in the Most Holy Blessed Sacrament, I ask thee to come into my heart, and make it like thy heart. *Amen.*

PRAYER TO MY GUARDIAN ANGEL

Angel of God, my guardian dear, To whom God's love commits me here, Ever this day be at my side, To light and guard, to rule and guide. *Amen.*

Art Credits

PHOTOGRAPHS

7 gifts of the holy spirit

2 Knowledge
1 Wisdom
6 fortitude ★ (Fear of the Lord)
7 piety
5 council
3 Understanding
4 Courage

1) Baptism - (Introduce to Gods Family
2) Confirmation - (seals us and light us on fire
3) Eucharistic - (Food for our soul)
3) Annoynting of the sick (heels you spiritually and physically)
5) confession - (kick the bad out and let god in)
6) holy Order - (are the minister)
7) Marriage - (creating a new life)